DURHAM
CATHEDRAL ORGANS

Richard Hird
and
James Lancelot

The Dean and Chapter of Durham
First Printing 1991
Re-printings 1994 and 2000
Fourth printing, with amendments, 2014

ISBN 978-1-907981-06-7

Cover illustrations:
Front cover: South case of the organ, seen through the Scott Screen [© C.R.A.Davies]
Back cover: Cartoon for the E. Hastings painting of Assizes Sunday [reproduced courtesy of the Cathedral Chapter]

Published by Durham Cathedral Chapter with the Cathedral Choir Association [DCCA], and printed and bound in England by B & B Press (Parkgate) Ltd.

About the authors

Richard Hird, who has written here about the organs in the Cathedral to 1876 and their fates, has lived in Durham since 1976, and before retirement was professionally employed in Planning. He has spent a lifetime pursuing an interest studying organs, their makers and history, acquiring a widespread and detailed knowledge, as well as being much occupied in playing and administration. For many years he has been a member of the Diocesan Advisory Committee for the Care of Churches and Diocesan Organs Adviser, and is a former longtime Treasurer and Council member and now an Organ Register Editor for the British Institute of Organ Studies, as well as being current President of Darlington Organists' Association. His contribution here is one of several authoritative studies and published articles – each evidence of a broad understanding and an absorbing and caring concern for these subjects.

James Lancelot, who has written about the history of the present organ from 1876 onwards, and provides a fulsome appreciation, was appointed Master of the Choristers and Organist of Durham Cathedral in 1985. Prior to this he was successively a chorister of St. Paul's Cathedral, Organ Scholar at King's College, Cambridge, and ten years Sub-Organist of Winchester Cathedral. He studied with Ralph Downes, Gillian Weir, and Nicholas Danby, taking ARCO aged 15 in 1968, FRCO in 1969 and CHM in 1971. At Durham he takes responsibility for the Cathedral's musical ministry, the centuries old tradition of music at the heart of Cathedral worship, with the two Cathedral choirs naturally taking much of his working time and energy. He is also in demand as a recitalist throughout Britain and abroad, and has many renowned recordings on CD and DVD to his credit. In 2002 James became a Lay Canon of the Cathedral, also receiving an Honorary Fellowship of the Guild of Church Musicians, and is University Organist – the University conferring an Honorary Doctorate of Music in summer 2014. He was awarded an Honorary Fellowship of the Royal School of Church Music in 2008, and is currently [2014] President of the Incorporated Association of Organists.

Durham Cathedral organs

Contents

Durham Cathedral organs

Introduction

For some time the authors have had in mind to re-write the story of Durham Cathedral's organs and are grateful to the Dean and Chapter for the opportunity to publish the fruits of their labours. Since Conrad Eden's booklet *Organs Past and Present in Durham Cathedral* was prepared and first published in 1970, 'organ studies' have developed. New sources have been discovered and a great deal of further delving in the Cathedral and organ-builders' own archives and elsewhere has verified many facts, but also revealed a significant quantity of additional information. This more recent study, with some thoughtful re-interpretation, challenges many established 'truths', provides extra detail, and throws fresh light on this important aspect of the Cathedral's history. Perhaps even, there are some lessons for the future?

We are especially thankful to (the late) Mr. Tony Davies for his excellent photographs, used, with continued permission, to illustrate this booklet; Mr. Mark Venning, now Chairman, and Harrison & Harrison Ltd for assistance sourcing new photographs and with stop lists; to Dr. Brian Crosby for providing the lists of Masters of the Choristers and Organists – the outcome of his own researches – and to (the late) Mr. Michael Gillingham for his learned contribution relating to the present organ cases.

Particular thanks are also due to those who have willingly assisted our task, and who were prepared to discuss if not always answer innumerable queries – Mr. Roger Norris (formerly) of the Chapter Library, Messrs Pat Mussett and (the late) Alan Piper (formerly) of the University Library; Miss Beth Rainey, (formerly) Keeper of Rare Books in the University Library; Miss Jennifer Gill, (former) County Archivist; Messrs Malcolm Jones and David Wickens, (former) honorary Archivists at the British Organ Archive in Birmingham; and also (the late) Dr. Michael Sayer, its former Archivist, for first discovering the Durham entries in the Hill and Gray & Davison records, and others too numerous, whom we trust will forgive us for any offence at not being mentioned. All errors in the booklet, whether of omission or commission, are however our own.

Clearly in a work of this scope and character, we are unable always to give precise references to all the documents and sources used. In order that our efforts may be available for reference and so that questions arising at any time may start on the same factual basis, a more fully annotated version of the booklet, together with other background material, will be deposited in the Chapter Library.

An assembly of parts of the west front of the Father Smith case and its supporting screen, as reconstructed in the South nave aisle [© RDH].

1
Organs prior to 1873

Writing a concise yet accurate history of an ancient Cathedral's organs is an unenviable task. Sorting fact from rumour or fiction can be a time-consuming and thankless exercise, but made a little surer at Durham with the wealth of manuscript records spanning the Cathedral's monastic and later history. Historians have often pored over these documents, but never before it appears with the primary purpose of writing the full story of the Cathedral's organs. Particular documents - such as the Agreement of 1683 [Appendix 1] - are very well known and frequently quoted, but it seems that earlier writers either had access to only a limited range of documents, or they simply picked on information readily found, or relied on secondary sources, without directly seeking or consulting the originals. Accordingly, the story of the organs has developed piecemeal, from incomplete, inconsistent and sometimes less than accurate sources, with an element of speculation to paper over the cracks.

In writing this new booklet, the authors have sought to avoid supposition and second-hand information by referring (so far as practicable within the resources and limited time at their disposal) to a wide range of available documents in the first instance, or to trusted secondary sources, and other real evidence. Inevitably the later records and evidence are more comprehensive and reliable, and so less liable to misinterpretation. This also explains the balance of the booklet, for one cannot write about what is not recorded in the early days, yet must carefully select the more interesting or relevant details from the past 150 years, when there is an overwhelming amount of information in many different sources from which to choose.

The early history

It would take a lifetime to peruse all the early records of the Priory Church and monastery of St. Cuthbert, and so we must rely to a large extent on the painstaking transcripts of antiquarians. Prior Darlington is reported as making a large tower and "organa grandiora" for the Priory during his tenure 1258 to 1272 or 1286 to 1290. The use here of "organa" is not certain, and may mean "works" or "more splendour" rather than a pipe organ as such. You may choose therefore whether to believe on this basis that there was an organ, however simple, for use "alternatim" with the plainchant used in the services in this building 725 or so years ago. A Priory's organ may have been built by the monks, or possibly by itinerants (building for Benedictine monasteries throughout the country, or Europe), but we shall probably never know!

There are however a number of references to organs in the Priory Account Rolls over the next 200 years:-

1334	12d for playing the organs at the feast of Easter
1377/8	D'no Reginald de Wermouth *ad facturam organorum* - 10s
1378/9	*In reparacione organorum* - 3s 4d
1425/6 & 1435/6	*Ad facturum organorum* - 6s 8d

Prior Wessington [1416-46] expended £26 13s 4d *in factura diversorum parium organorum*.

In his booklet *Durham Cathedral: Choristers and their Masters* (1980) Brian Crosby has identified other references - for the purchase of an organ book in 1387/8, payment in 1416/7 to the Cantor for instructing youths on the organ, and to the "Master of the Organ". In December 1430, in his detailed Contract with the Priory, a new Cantor was required to give instruction in playing the organ, and (even though a layman) was needed to play the organ or sing for services in the Quire as directed by the Precentor.

There is also a very full and descriptive account - written in retrospect - of the life and appearance of the Priory Church before its Dissolution in 1539 – the *Rites of Durham*. Fowler's edition of 1902 provides a complete transcript and commentary upon the various versions. Davies's 1672 edition of the *Rites* is dedicated to James Mickleton of Durham, and Mickleton's own annotated copy is now in the University Library's collections. Clearly his comments are a useful and near contemporary source of information about happenings at the Cathedral and of its organs. It is from the *Rites* that we learn that there were 5 organs sited and used in different parts of the Priory church before the Dissolution:

> The Quire - "there was 3 paire of organs belonginge to the said quire ... one of the fairest paire of the three did stand ouer the quire dore only opened and playd uppon at principall feastes, the pipes beinge all of most fine wood and workmanshipp uerye faire, partly gilted uppon the inside and the outside of the leaves [doors] and couers up to the topp with branches and flowers finely gilted with the name of Jesus gilted with gold: there was but 2 paire more of them in all England of the same makinge, one paire in Yorke and another in Paules [St. Paul's]".

> "The second paire stood on the north side of the quire beinge neuer playd uppon but when the 4 doctors of the church was read ... beinge a faire paire of large organs called the cryers". "The third paire was daily used at ordinary service" - the "White" organ, possibly moveable, but based at the south side towards the vestry.

> The Nave - there was a "paire" before the Jesus altar in the nave, in a gallery on the north side, "for ye mr. and quiristers to sing Jesus mess euy fridaie".

> The Galilee - in this chapel at the west end of the building was "a paire of faire orgainis".

We are told that each Corpus Christi Day there was a procession from St. Nicholas's Church [in the Market Place] to the Cathedral, where a solemn service with the Te Deum was sung, accompanied by the organ. The Master of the Choir was contracted also to play the organ at High Mass and Evensong on special days; however when the monks sang Matins [the midnight service] one of their own number played the organ.

[For those unfamiliar with the term: "a paire of organs", what is meant is one organ (cf. a pair of scissors). In the time since this book was first written, the Wetheringsett and smaller Wingfield replica Tudor [Early English Organ Project] organs have been built, based upon documentary sources and evidence derived from real surviving fragments and known aspects of old organs; these organs were installed and used in Durham Cathedral over two extended periods, allowing a better appreciation of the organs and church music of those early times (http://www.goetzegwynn.co.uk/tudor.shtml)]

Post-Reformation organs

The monastery was dissolved at the end of 1539, but the foundation was reconstituted under a Dean and Chapter (rather than Prior and monks) and in many administrative respects then continued much as before. The next century was one of political manoeuvering between High Church and later Laudian views, which encouraged liturgy and music, and the Puritan ethic, which didn't; the organs fared accordingly.

The new Cathedral Statutes required that a Master "shall be elected, a man of honest report, of upright life, skilled in singing and playing the organs...".

There are passing references to the Cathedral organs in the records:-

1545	1 seven fawdome of cordes to ye organs - 6/8d
1557/8	1 payre bandes to ye organs - 8d
1569	At Masses held in the Cathedral at the time of the Rising of the North, John Brymley played the organ "in the loft over the quier door", and was subsequently called to account, but afterwards he was reconciled and no action was taken against him.
1577/8	Paid to Thackewrai for mending ye organs - 26/8d
Sept.1589	Wm. Smythe [petty canon; later organist] repaired "one pare of orgaynes wch. standeth above the Quere doore...yeld[ing] the most principallist & imperiall sound of all the rest...and haith not bene played upon thes many yeres for lacke of mendinge" - Alloc[ated] xxxs
July 1593 to Feb. 1594	Mr. Broughe was paid £12/12/0 "for altering and amending of the organes" involving, to according to the description, winching down the organ and taking it away to the Peti [ie. Minor] Canons' Hall. He was "involved in labour and great paynes with their great orgaines".
	[Broughe seems to have been nationally known, for in 1590 he was paid £8 at St. Margaret's Westminster "for changeing of our organs for a payre of his"].
1595	i plaite de ferro pro le stoppes cor[un]d[em] organor[um] - 1d
Mar.1600	To Robert Coup for ye key + string of ye organ - 6d
Sept.1610	To Thomas Coates for "revewing ye organs" - 13/4d
Nov. 1613	To Thomas Coates for "mending both the orgaines" - £5/6/8d
	[Danyell Coates and later a "Mr. Coots" appear in relation to organs in the Houghton le Spring parish records at the beginning of the 17th century; in 1635 Thomas Coats (sic) of Stamford was granted a pension for maintaining the organ in Lincoln Cathedral.]

Articles against Durham Innovators, a vitriolic broadsheet penned in 1630 by Puritan Canon Peter Smart and directed particularly at John Cosin [who favoured elaborate ritual; a prebendary or canon from 1624 until he was deprived and escaped to Paris in 1642], tells us:-

"You gave to the late Bishop of Durham a payre of organs, though not so gay [as the 1621 organ], yet as good as any Cathedral church had or hathe in the province of Yorke; you gave him them to gett his approbation of all your new ceremonies, which organes have been carried to London and there set to sale".

Supporting this there is a Chapter Order in 1622: "Graunted the right honorable the lord Bpp. of Duresme [Neile] one of the lesser organes in the Church and he to make Choise of the saide organe". He would seem to have taken the "Cryers", as the "White" organ stayed and (according to Mickleton) was witnessed played on in 1635 and 1636.

Thomas Dallam built a new organ on the screen ("over the Choir door") in late 1621, but there are only general references to it. It was paid for by the Dean with income from a lease of property. In November 1621 this organ was "lately begunne". It appears to be this instrument which is the subject of public comment. Smart's *Articles* in 1630 accuse: "You have built a new payre of gorgius organes which have cost at least 700li [lire=£]". An account by touring army officers visiting the City in 1634 says: "We were wrapt with the sweet sound and richnesse of a fayre organ, which cost £1000...".

There are more detailed records elsewhere of organs Thomas Dallam built early in the 17th century - for example at Kings College, Cambridge [costing £371] – current thinking suggests this was at the east end, rather than on the screen as today - Worcester Cathedral [£381], the Chapel Royal, Holyrood, Edinburgh [£300]. The cost of these two manual instruments it seems did not include their cases, built by different skilled craftsmen. Allowing for work done "about the organ" doubled the overall price to £609 at York Minster, an organ built by Thomas's son Robert in 1634. This, given an element of exaggeration, is not far short of the alleged cost of Dallam senior's Durham instrument. These instruments were similar in concept, harking to the Italianate tradition - that at York having 9 stops on the Great and 5 on the Choir, whilst the Worcester organ had one less stop on the Great. Such instruments have been described as "of some musical potential, stunted by political and puritan developments, but promising" so far as they went. There is no reason to think that the senior Dallam's organ for Durham would be greatly different. More information may come to light some day.

A somewhat different picture is given in Chapter Minutes, for in April 1628 we read of the Organist: "In regard of Richard Hutchinson frequent haunting of Aile houses and Divers other his evill demeaners, and especially for the breaking of the head of Toby Broking one of the Singing men of this church with a Candlesticke in an Ailehouse wounding him verie dangerously....". He was warned that time, but a month later was suspended to mend his ways! Organists also had other than the Dean and Chapter to contend with, for the Minutes tell us that in Jan.1632 Cuth[bert] Pattesi [or "Pattison"], the *organorum inflatori*, was paid 1/- for "catching rats in ye organ loft". £6/18/4d was paid for tuning the organ on 11th April 1632.

The end of the era of the Priory, the spirit of which had continued after the Dissolution, was near. Britain was in the throes of a Civil War. The Dean and Chapter fled at the coming of the Calvinist Scots in September 1640. Mickleton reminiscing 50 years later says that at first no harm was done, but on Midsummer Day 1641, until the intervention of one of their leaders, the iconoclast invaders started to vandalise the organs. So upon the advice of the Scottish General, during the next night the pipes were surreptitiously removed by Cathedral staff, for safekeeping. The surviving cases, with all other woodwork in the Cathedral except the Clock, were however burnt by Scottish troops imprisoned in the building in 1650. The Cathedral interior was wrecked and its establishment in chaos.

The Restoration

Ten years elapsed before the Restoration of the monarchy and the church in 1660. James Mickleton's personal recollections in his annotations to the *Rites* become a closely contemporary source. Writing only 30 years later he tells us that:-

> Organs "were brought into the Church in Bishop Cosin's time, to witt a pair of little organs that cost towards 80 pound, that came from London and (were) placed on the South side in a little loft towards the vestry which was made fitt for them and they were set up in ye sd loft in June and July 1661 ..."

Patently this was a temporary arrangement, for Chapter on October 5th 1661, ie. later that same year, ratified Articles made between the Dean and George Dallam of the Parish of St. Andrew in the Wardrobe, London, Organ-maker, on the 3rd July [perhaps he was setting up the small organs] - a bargain made with the assistance and approval of Bishop Cosin - to make and set up a faire double organ for £550 (£100 in advance).

There is a stop list of a Dallam-style organ of 13 stops, no reeds, written in the hand of John Foster (Organist 1661 - 1677) in the flyleaf of one of the contemporary Anthem Books:-

In the great organ	Stops in the Chair organ
1. open diopasion	1. the principall
2. the ist principall	2. a 15th
3. the 2 principall	3. a 22th
4. the stopt diopasion	4. a diopasan [stopt]
5. the 15	5. the flut [at the octave]
6. the 12	
7. the 22th	
8. the furnoture	

Mickleton also records an incident - that the new "pair of Great organs ... were finished ... against Christmas 1662, but were not played on at Christmasse Day, but the little organs were played on; at which Dean Sudbury was angry, but after, on St. Stephen's Day, the said Great organs were first played on by Mr. John Foster Organist and so continued to be played on". There is a reference elsewhere to the keys to the "Great organ door" being with "Mr.ffoster".

It seems the "little organs" were disposed of. An Inventory of 1665 notes: "Two paire of organs", though an added comment records "one paire of them is latily sold to Houghton [le Spring]". There, according to the Churchwardens' Accounts, several payments were made for liquid refreshment when "the organs came home" in 1665.

In churches, old organs which were put back at the Restoration, or indeed as at Durham, many new organs which had been built perhaps in rather too much haste, were soon replaced. The pre-Commonwealth traditions of organ-building had resumed at the Restoration. Organ-builders (even the Dallams, who had continued organ-building in Brittany and must have assimilated new methods and styles there) and their patrons in the church hierarchy (who perhaps knew no different) reverted to ways which now seem idiosyncratic, but were geared to choral accompaniment. It seems that many organs were what are now termed "transposing organs" - ie. notes sounded at a different pitch relative to that played (a fourth higher - choir pitch, or a fifth lower - organ pitch)*. Curious as it may seem today, there is increasingly sufficient evidence generally to show that such instruments were built in Britain after the Commonwealth. This convention was taken for granted, so proof is scattered and often sketchy, and there is no certainty that this is the reason George Dallam's organ at Durham survived only 23 years. Father Smith, when he erected his new organ, obtained the old one, but thought "to mak it a good organ will cost monnes". It was only with the passing of one generation of organ builders, and changes in style introduced by their successors, that the curious transposing system was outmoded.

* Note: the lower and upper keyboards controlled, respectively, a Chair or Choir organ having C as its lowest key playing a pipe of 5ft speaking length (ie. sounding the note bass F) with keyboard compass of about 4 octaves reflecting vocal range, and a Great organ, keyboard layout and usual pitch an octave lower. A choral piece in the key of C, for instance, would be written out for, and/or played by the organist in key G.

The Father Smith organ

Bernard ("Father") Smith's organ for Durham Cathedral was exceptional. He described it as "so goode and sound mad as anny is in the holl worrelt" and "for ferriety of stopes and quarter nots that no organ has but yours and in the Temply [Temple Church, London] that I made". Much is known of this organ and its subsequent history right through to 1873, the year of its demise.

Schemes for a new Cathedral organ were submitted in 1683 by two rival builders who were responsible for most of the output of organs in Britain for nearly 50 years - Father Smith (his scheme to cost £700 plus the old organ) and the Harrises (father Thomas - not in the best of health - and son Renatus; their proposals to cost £670 plus the old organ). The proposed number of stops was the same in each scheme. The Harrises would have mutations and mixtures, but no reeds except for an optional Vox Humana - surprising, because it has always been said that Harris made better reeds. Perhaps after experience building an organ at St. Nicholas's Newcastle upon Tyne in 1676 they thought the provinces not ready for innovation, or more probably, that reeds would not be adequately maintained so far from London. It is the case however that the Agreement with Smith had been signed on the 18th August and the first payment had been made before the Harrises' speculative proposals, dated 28th August, were penned (sent to Durham with a letter dated 30th August)!

The Articles of Agreement between Smith and the Dean and Chapter make interesting reading and so are transcribed in full for reference elsewhere in this booklet. This contract required the new organ to be set up before 1st May 1685. Payment was to be made in three installments of £233/6/8d, the first at the signing of the Agreement, the second when the organ was brought to the Cathedral and the third at satisfactory completion. Painting and gilding of the two fronts was to be "at the proper cost and charges of" Smith, but if he did well in making, finishing and fitting up the new organ, an additional £50 was to be paid for this decoration work.

The second payment (due on delivery) both the Audit Book and Smith's receipt show was not made until September 21st 1685, once Dean Granville was "satisfied that all ye materials of ye organ are...placed". The third was made in 1686 (actual date unspecified in the Audit Book). Smith was still working in Durham in July 1686, writing a letter to the Dean of Canterbury from Durham then. Mickleton reporting in 1691 recalls that the organ "was set up and finished in August 86".

There are other documents - letters and papers - in the Cathedral records still, which seem to show that the organ built was bigger and more complicated than that specified in the Agreement. Negotiations over what Smith alleged were his extra costs, continued by letter from London in November 1686 and December 1687. The first letter, as we have seen from the quotation at the beginning of this section, clarifies that enharmonic keyboards were installed from the outset. A later paper headed "Mr. Smithe addition to yee organ beyond contract" confirms that there were 7 extra pipes in each rank - a d sharp and g sharp, distinct from e flat and a flat, in each octave except the lowest. The divided Great soundboard and roller board, with Smith markings, survived throughout the organ's life; Dr. Armes, who was involved in its final dismantling, notes in correspondence that these extra pipes had occupied their place in sequence on the soundboard. Provision for intervals smaller than a semitone allowed for more perfect tuning in "remote" keys, which were otherwise difficult to achieve in the days before "modern" equal temperament was introduced. An example of a 17th century virginals with "quarter notes" - the key is split, the back part raised higher than the front - may be seen in the Russell Collection in Edinburgh. As one writer put it, such a relatively unusual arrangement required "a person well acquainted with this peculiar keyboard to avail himself of its use", and it is interesting to find that William Greggs, the Durham organist, was given leave for three months in 1686 "to goe to London to improve himself in the Skill of Musicke".

In a later letter Smith cites "...the quantity of more worck then there was a greed fore"; these "additions beyond contract" are found in the records as a written out stop list of the organ built - different from that in the earlier Agreement in that it includes a III rank Sesquialtera and an extra rank in the Mixture, but no separate Blockflute on the Great of 12 stops, and a Two & Twenty, making 6 stops on the Chaire. The complete stop list, with further stop lists of the Smith organ as subsequently altered and developed, is presented in tabular form in the Appendices to this book.

Somewhat quaintly Smith argues that he had "out gon the pris...I declare that it cost mee a bove a thousent pound...for the will chorn [ie. Chapter will scorn] to see mee a loser, aldo the contrack be other wayes"; also that he "receeved the hondert and fifty pound yesterday" [though it has to be said that there is no such amount recorded in the Audit Book - just the final installment amount]. It could be that some of the final payment was withheld for some reason in 1686, but why then is the full installment (and only that amount) shown in the Audit Book? If both amounts were paid, had Chapter accepted Smith's comments about underpayment, and who paid the extra? In that case, by late 1686 had Smith received altogether £850 and made a little bit more [£20] by re-using the old Choir organ [though he replaced 4 out of the 5 ranks] at the Popish Chapel in York?

The following year was paid "To Mr. Smith the organmaker: £50/0/0" - presumably the extra promised in the Agreement if the work and decorating the fronts were well done - and "To his nephew: £5/7/6". Responding, Smith commented that the £50 "has ben dew a grat whill sins...I did ex peckt an other kind of sum", but the pleadings fell on deaf ears.

Smith's grumblings over the real cost of the organ seem to have continued. The "additions beyond contract" manuscript, dated 1690, is Smith accounting for the extras. As the document goes on to say after the stoplist: "...it is not only the pipes [352] that is addision, it is also in the soundbord, rolingbord, keas, and in all musements [movements] which comes to a Grat deall of work, and considering the addision in the front pipes and painting comes to a Grat deal more then the a Greement".

Tradition, promulgated by Sir John Sutton in *A short account of organs* (1847), had it that "an addition was made a few years after it was set up, by Schmidt himself, and from the number of pipes introduced, it seems not improbable that this was an Echo". Other subsequent writers have used Sutton's little speculation to jump to the conclusion that Smith added a third manual or at least some extra stops in 1690 or '91. But if Sutton and later imitators thought that it was the extra stops and quarter tones from the "beyond contract" manuscript which had been added in 1690 then that cannot be right.

Father Smith certainly was in Durham in 1690, and in the first instance was paid three small amounts totalling £26, hardly sufficient for major work. Oddly however Chapter then "Ordered to Mr. Ber'd Smth twenty four pounds, wh. with the twenty six placed to this above written account amounts guift [given] to him this Audit and in all £50". If Smith was still arguing about the original cost of the organ with the Chapter, through the Chapter Clerk, then it seems he was partially successful and did manage to recoup a little more to offset his losses. Immediately following in the Audit Book is the entry "Ordered to Mr. Wilson [the Registrar] for his extraordinary services to the Chapter this year £20" - one wonders if Wilson had been awkward in negotiations!

Smith accepted the additional £24 as "being the last payment and in full" and satisfaction appears to have been achieved more than seven years after the signing of the original Agreement.

What of Father Smith and this, arguably one of his finest organs? Bernard Smith, though justifiably famous as an organ-builder, remains something of an enigma. His renown and aura were such that many old organs came to be "by Father Smith", and it is only in recent years that more thorough researches have revealed more of the man, his life and work, and scotched some of the myths. The earliest documentary evidence appears in relation to tuning at Westminster Abbey in 1667, and it seems Smith came to London from the Netherlands after the Great Fire, at the age of 37 or 38. There are several theories about his origins, which now suggest he was born and trained in north Germany, but moved to Holland in 1657. His great rivals the Harrises brought a French influence on their return at the Restoration, but Smith brought Dutch/German ideas. Even so the British organ remained insular and idiosyncratic, only conservatively modified from earlier traditions, musical but with limitations, and generally smaller than and very different to its European contemporaries.

Smith was permitted to import tools for repairs to the organ in the Chapel Royal, Whitehall in 1671, and had continuing contact with the Court, but was not properly appointed Organ Maker to the King until 1681. He became organist at St. Margaret, Westminster in 1676 and moved in influential circles. Andrew Freeman's book *Father Smith* (1926), with annotations and additions by John Rowntree (1976), lists some 120 places with organs ascribed with different degrees of certainty to Smith, who died in February 1708. Best known and largest of his instruments, as well as Durham, are those at the Temple Church (successful in the "Battle of the Organs" against Renatus Harris's instrument and also possessing quarter notes) and St. Paul's.

There is a paucity of his work remaining; a few cabinet organs which may well be his work remain relatively unscathed, but of the larger instruments some noble cases survive, but little of their content has escaped the hand of "improvers" or replacement over the years. Accordingly it is difficult to comment on what the Durham Cathedral organ actually was like and how it would have sounded. Even 18th and 19th century writers complained that "there are very few [Smith instruments] remaining in their original state". They do tell of "the equality and sweetness of his stops, as well as the soundness of his pipes", though "the [key] touch is the worst part...and is very disagreeable to those unaccustomed to play upon them, feeling as though cotton wool was placed under each key". The bellows – hand blown of course - are said to have supplied the wind in a very irregular manner, causing the organs to sound tremulous. "The great beauty ... consists in the sweetness and brilliancy of the wooden pipes ... the chorus is also very fine and very brilliant in effect" but without shrillness. "Every note tells and the bass is very firm and speaks decidedly", and the tone was even throughout the compass. Smith himself talks of "all that keer and pains" he had taken over his Durham opus - "it dus not bare the truble of it". Smith took care with his use of materials, and though a pipe was said to "look like the devil", he could "make it speak like an angel"; it is said that his fineness of tone has never been equalled, though Sutton reported that all Smith's reed stops "are very coarse".

Metal pipes he could make speak like those made of wood, and those of wood to speak like those of metal! Dean Kitchin's Report on the remains of the Durham organ says Smith's metal pipes are of the composition tin to lead 16:6 [sic]. However, an analysis by Harrison & Harrison revealed the opposite, 25% tin to 75% lead, in line with normal English practice for non-show pipes, but less "rich" than Jordan's metal (1748) where the analysis showed the proportion of tin was 33%.

Obviously this celebrated organ-builder set new standards - as a clever master craftsman, though his mechanisms were not the best, and a great tonal artist. The evidence here that he far exceeded the agreed price and hoped that "the Dean and Chapter will not see mee a loser" perhaps suggests that it was as a practical and careful organ-builder that Smith excelled, and not as a businessman! It is from the records and descriptions that one can try to judge the character, condition and quality of Father Smith's fine Durham organ. Arguably his concepts and skills established the form of instrument that is understood and could be used today.

Eighteenth century consolidation

After the turmoil of the previous century the Cathedral establishment settled down to gracious normality, its routines organised and its way of life largely undisturbed for a century and a half. The Dean and Chapter Minute Books and Accounts provide an irrefutable and contemporary record of instructions and expenditure relating to the Smith organ, never before fully revealed. Secondary sources will only be used to supplement and compare information where there are conflicts or shortcomings.

In the first 50 years there was notable expense only twice; in 1711, after the appointment of James Heseltine as the new organist, we find "Church Organ: £120", and two years later "To ye organ maker: £20". There is no evidence, but it seems likely that Gerard Smith, who we have heard was involved with his uncle when the organ was built, may well have been the organ-builder summoned, but for what reason is not specified. The amount is not small, but neither does it seem large enough for significant alterations. Probably repairs only were involved, but it is unwise to speculate! In August 1738, a sum of 5 gns. was paid "for mending ye organ", to Mr. Knople [a small-scale London organ-builder who signed a receipt at St.James, Garlickhythe - "Johann Knoppell"].

Jordan and Bridge

Innocuous though it appears, the agreement by Chapter on the 2nd November 1744 to "mending and cleaning the organ", foretells what seems to have been the first major alterations to the organ. Yet it was not until 1746 that payment [15gns] is made "To Mr. Jordan Organ Builder for his journey" to inspect and report. Payments for the work itself are made in two equal sums of £170 in 1747 and '48. Abraham Jordan senior had been responsible for introducing to English organ-building the novel idea of putting part of an organ, the sets of pipes controlled by one of the keyboards, into a box with a sliding front so that the sound could be "swelled". It was his son, however, Abraham junior, on his last assignment, whom it was said added a Swell division of four stops to the 60 year old Durham instrument.

In fact the work seems to have been undertaken by another already established London organ builder, Richard Bridge, presumably in collusion with, or subcontracted by Jordan. Chapter in November 1748 "agreed to give Mr. Bridge and the other two workmen at the organ 15gns conditionally that they tune the organ when they come into the country the next year" and "Mr. Bridges" was paid this amount "for extraordinary trouble at ye organ" in 1748, and a further 10gns "for mending the organ" in 1750.

True, the archives do not throw any light on the precise nature of the work carried out in 1748 and the best secondary sources - writing the following century - differ. Sperling, a savant whose Notebooks on organs of c.1850 are deposited in the British Library, seems first to have ascribed what he calls the "Echo" [of 5 stops] to Bridge, but then crossed that name out and substituted Jordan's. Hopkins & Rimbault in their tome *The Organ, its history and construction* (1855) say: "The instrument was repaired by Abraham Jordan in 1748, who is supposed to have added the Swell...". Buckingham, however, an organ-builder who himself looked after and altered the Durham organ in the 1820s and '30s and is normally a reliable source of information, seems to be out of step in suggesting that Snetzler added the Swell in 1765!

Snetzler

The appointment of Thomas Ebdon as organist in 1763 must have been a spur to further thoughts of modification. Minutes in November 1765 report that "Mr.Dean sent John Snetzler's proposals for repairing the organ which were agreed to"; £130 was paid to "Mr.Snetzler for cleaning and repairing the organ". Of the various other sources both Buckingham's Diary and Sperling recognise that Snetzler did work at Durham. Buckingham tells us that an 8ft and a 4ft Dulciana - a popular new type of soft stop developed by this builder - were introduced into the Choir or Chaire division, and the Choir 4ft Flute "all through of metal" - capped, with chimneys, according to Dr. Armes writing in 1880 - was substituted for Smith's wooden one.

Donaldson

The next organbuilder to be associated with the instrument is believed to have worked for Snetzler before setting up business on his own account, first in Newcastle, later in York. The appearance of John Donaldson's name in the Durham 1780/1 accounts is a helpful find, preceding all other known examples of his work. As usual Chapter simply "Agreed that that organ be repaired and cleaned" [27th October 1780]; Donaldson's "Bill for repairing the organ" then was £42/5/6d. There are further expenditures for repairs, notably £32/18/10d in 1792 and 16gns in 1796, but not attributed.

The nineteenth century – time of change

At the turn of the century, though there is no discussion recorded, Chapter must have thought of major changes to the interior as well as the exterior of the Cathedral. James Wyatt, the Architect, was commissioned in 1795 and a portfolio of remarkable drawings survives. Among these are two, one of an east elevation, the other being a west elevation of an organ curiously utilising as its cases a reconstruction of the mediaeval stone reredos, the Neville screen. Wyatt wished to dispose of the wooden Restoration screen with surmounting organ that divided Quire from Nave, opening up the through vista, substituting the re-assembled Neville screen cum organ case to the east of the

Quire. For whatever reason, probably their radicalism, and undoubted cost, most of the architect's "improvements" here never materialised. The Father Smith organ escaped.

Avery

Nevertheless the organ soon demanded further attention, and in 1802, £199/7/-, and in 1804 £32 was spent on "Repairs at the organ". The probable contractor is revealed in correspondence between the Bishop of Lichfield and the Dean of Durham, which seeks and obtains information about the capacity of John Avery to repair the organ. The nature of the Chapter's caution is disclosed in an anecdote given in *Musical Memoirs* by W. Parke (1830):

> "... having called on that celebrated musician, Doctor Arnold, at his house in Duke Street, Westminster, our conversation was interrupted by the arrival of Mr. A---y, the organ builder, a man of irregular habits, who came on business. 'How do you get on now?' asked the Doctor. 'Oh' said Mr. A---y, 'Very well. I work hard all day, and go to bed happy at night'. 'Ay' said the Doctor, 'We can all go to bed happy at night, but the test is how we arise in the morning!' ".

Sir John Sutton is less subtle - "Avory [sic] who was a shocking drunken character, and a person not in any way to be depended upon, being generally drunk and often in prison for debt, was nevertheless an excellent workman, when he was once set to work ..".

England and Nicholls

Again immediately upon the arrival of a new organist - William Henshaw in 1813 - follows major work to the organ. In June 1814, Chapter agreed that "Mr. England be immediately employed to clean and tune the organ" and the accounts for the following year uncover the cost, £343/15/4d, plus £5/1/3d for "carriage of goods from London by Waggon, for repairing the organ in 1815". During the course of the work George Pike England died, and so the work was completed by his son-in-law, William Nicholls. Afterwards Chapter "Agreed that Mr. Wm. Nichols [sic] be engaged annually to tune the organ in the Quire at 10gns per annum each time, including expenses of journey", though in 1820 he was "dismissed" and it was agreed that another tuner be got. Further repairs costing £40/10/- are recorded in 1817.

The later sources generally corroborate each other, confirming that England/Nicholls's work was quite extensive. A Principal 4ft and Cornet III ranks were reported added to the Swell [although a Durham manuscript stoplist pre-dating the England work shows a Cornet already on the "Echoes"], and a Cremona replaced the Vox Humana on the Choir. Other reed stops were "renewed", a Double Diapason of 24 pipes on the Great and a set of 17 "toe pedals" added, the pitch lowered and the top end of the compass extended. These latter two changes it seems were effected in part by suppressing the quarter notes, disconnecting their action and presumably removing superfluous pipes, but utilising then available soundboard space. Dr. Armes in 1880 describes spare pipe holes on the surviving Great soundboard as "patched over with strips of parchment". The old keyboards formerly displayed in the Monks' Dormitory, though altered, are those provided in 1815.

Buckingham

It is not long before Buckingham provides a first hand account of the Cathedral organ as he found it. Alexander Buckingham built a few small instruments, but principally traveled the country looking after existing ones. He described himself as "Foreman to the late Mr. Avery and Mr. Elliot", but it may be that his introduction to Durham arose when installing the Song School organ by James Davis in August 1821, described elsewhere in this book. Though his Notebook entry for Durham - the first in the series - is dated August 1823, in fact his name appears in the Durham

Elevation of the Organ Screen towards the Nave

Drawing for proposed new organ case: Wyatt, 1795
[reproduced courtesy of the Cathedral Chapter]

accounts in connection with the Cathedral organ the previous August, when he was paid 13gns for tuning, and then annually each summer for small cost work - tuning, repairs, cleaning. In 1832 Chapter "ordered that Mr. Buckingham do procure new bellows for the organ upon new and improved construction as proposed by him", and in August 1833 there is the payment of £62/12/- for this. A comment in the Notebook records "New Horizontal bellows added July 30th 1833 by A. Buckingham". Higher than normal annual payments reflect repairs and alterations undertaken by Buckingham in 1836 [£30] and 1840 [£88], when a Venetian Swell front replaced the "nag's head" arrangement and a coupler movement was added. Buckingham's final appearance in Durham was on the 29th July 1843.

Bishop

The coming of George Waddington as Dean in 1840 brought new ideas; he determined to render the Cathedral more accessible to the public for worship. The organ and wooden screen upon which it stood survived *in situ* for only a few more years. Chapter on the 20th November 1843, however, "Agreed that the Organ be repaired in the place where it now stands according to the first Report and estimate this day made by Mr. Bishop".

For completeness, before clarifying Bishop's scheme, it is important to reveal significant alternative proposals prepared by another firm. William Hill provided two propositions:

> <u>Durham Cathedral</u>   <u>Estimate Nov.7th [1843]</u>
>
> [A]   For a new Organ, to have 3 rows of keys + Pedal Organ. Great Organ keys to be carried (if thought proper) to CCC to act upon Pedal Organ
>
>   <u>Great Organ</u> CC to F   [15 stops]
>   Bourdon, Tenoroon, Open Dia, Stop Dia, Principal, Quint, 10th, 12th, 15th, 8ve 15, Sesquialtra, Mixture, Posaune, Clarion, U [ie.Unison] Flute.
>
>   <u>Choir Organ</u> CC to F   [8 stops]
>   Open Dia, Viol de Gambe, Stop Dia, Principal, Oboe Flute, 15th, Stop Flute, Cremona.
>
>   <u>Swell</u>, Gam G to F   [8 stops]
>   Double Dul, Open Dia, Stop Dia, Principal, 15th, Sesquialtra, Cornopean, Oboe,
>
>   <u>Pedal Org</u>. CCC to D   [6 stops]
>   Open Wood 16, D'o Metal 16, Principal 8, 15th, Sesquialtra V ranks, Trombone 16
>
>   <u>Copulas.</u> Sw to Gt, Ped to Gt, Ped to Ch.
>   3 composition Pedals to Great Organ and 2 to Pedal Organ.
>
>   The whole to be finished in the best manner, without case and carriage, for the sum of £850. A proper sum to be allowed for the Old Organ.
>
> [B]   To remove [relocate?] the Organ in Durham Cathedral, New Sw. Tenor C, New Pedal pipes CCC, compass extended from E to F, New pipes in Choir, 3 Composition pedals. £450.

William Hill was a strong influence in Victorian organ-building, and greatly responsible for changes in design arising out of ideas emanating from the Continent. Mendelssohn's London visits, when he played his own and Bach's works - and visited Durham - are recognised as the "missionary" influence. These occasions required organs with Pedals - available in either only rudimentary form, or not at all, in the British organs of the time. Durham's organ well illustrates the point! Hill, encouraged by H.J.Gauntlett - a promoter of the "German system" of standard C compass for all manuals and pedals, and of suitably developed Pedal divisions, rose to the challenge, not only in the provision of a Pedal of sufficient compass, with separate stops and capable of holding its own against the manuals, but in the introduction of new types of stop. Hill's scheme for Durham, is startling for its time. The Pedal division (with a full chorus and reed) and the Great (with its mutation series and two reeds) are pioneering in concept; the Choir and short compass Swell, perhaps for reasons of space or cost, are more traditional. Whatever their merits, the proposals for a new organ did not proceed, and a more conservative builder's proposals for modifying the existing instrument *in situ* were accepted.

Laurence Elvin [in *Bishop & Son, Organ Builders - the Story of J.C.Bishop and his successors* (1984)] has investigated and written about the life and work of J.C.Bishop, including time spent at Durham, in far more detail than can here be accommodated. The care of the Durham Cathedral organ was in the hands of this firm for over 20 years, from Chapter's acceptance of proposals for repairs in November 1843 until February 1864. Although described as a repair, the work undertaken in 1844 was substantial - sufficient for Sir John Sutton to proclaim "...the Writer cannot but think the additions lately made to this Organ unnecessary as the instrument was perfectly effective before". Many changes to the organ were made - new stops were introduced in place of "old fashioned" ones, and much new pipework substituted for old ranks. More specifically, the Swell organ compass was extended to Tenor C and a Clarion 4ft replaced the 1815 Cornet. On the Great Bishop substituted a short compass Clarabella for the Cornet and renewed the Twelfth, Tierce, Mixture and Sesquialtera. A new Stopped Diapason and Dulciana replaced the previous specimens on the Choir, whilst 24 "German" pedals [GG to g, no GG sharp] with an independent set of double Pedal Pipes replaced England's pull-down toe Pedals. Four new-fangled composition pedals were added. The Cathedral paid £523/6/3d to Bishop, together with some £108 for sundry associated work.

Dean Waddington's way was not long forthcoming however, involving the reordering of the whole Quire area. The oak organ screen - "boldly and not unskilfully carved, but after designs wholly inappropriate to a place of worship" - was removed in 1847. The organ was relocated east of the stalls, on the north side facing the Bishop's Throne. The purpose is explained in the Chapter Minute of September 1846: "The Report from Mr. Bishop respecting the removal of the organ with the view of making the space to the west of the skreen [sic] available for the purposes of worship was presented...". The decision to go ahead was made at Great Chapter in February 1847, when the Dean made Chapter a generous offer; he would settle the account himself and help pay the cost of the organ's return and for a new screen if Chapter resolved to restore the status quo after the trial period. But by November that year it was the opinion of Chapter that the success of the alterations which had been carried into effect "was fully proved".

Others thought differently, as is reflected in S.S.Wesley's view in 1863: "On the late excellent organ builder, Mr. Bishop, being summoned to Durham Cathedral to move the organ from the centre to the side of the choir, I was induced to inquire of him how he, a conscientious man, and friend to music, could be party to so scandalous an act as that of ruining the effect of both the organ and the Choir-service for all future times. He replied thus – 'I may as well do the job now, for if I don't somebody else will. Depend on this; we shall soon have to put all the organs back again'. This has however not yet proved true. The organs are not put back, and architects are still successful in their inexcusable efforts to displace our cathedral and other church organs ... it is not always so easy to correct, soon, a bad fashion".

J.C.Bishop sent his account for £420, comprising £250 for dismantling and re-erection, £100 for necessary alterations, and most of the balance for transposing the pitch and re-voicing. Bishop's records show a replacement Cremona and Hautboy were not charged for. As the Dean paid, the amount does not appear in the Chapter accounts. An early photograph shows the organ in this position; the whole organ sits on the floor, with the Chaire organ projecting into the Quire. To fit the limited width between the pillars the two side towers of the "east" main case were removed leaving a pathetic mutilation. The "west" case presumably was crammed in the aisle. The new position seems to have brought with it new problems, particularly of damp, affecting leather, wood and glue; problems were dealt with almost annually by the firm both before and after Bishop's death in December 1854.

More significant expenditure was encountered in 1859. Chapter Minutes report that "A representation having been made by Mr. Henshaw that the old Choir organ was nearly useless and estimates having been sent in by Bishop & Co. for a new Choir organ with two additional stops at a cost of 100gns agreed that the same be ordered accordingly". The firm provided a new Choir soundboard for the old one "being quite worn out", adding an Open Diapason and Viol di Gamba, both Tenor C stops, a Suboctave coupler Choir to Great, cleaning and repairs - all in the sum of £150/3/-. A further £42 was expended in early 1861 on the account of Bishop Starr & Richardson.

When Philip Armes was appointed organist following Henshaw's retirement in 1862, palliatives were sought by having the organ tuned to equal temperament, adding two more couplers, which with cleaning, between July 1863 and February 1864, cost altogether £75 - the final payment to Mr. C.A. Bishop. Armes, writing in 1883, however, thought little of Bishop's work, describing his pipework as "just the ordinary type of the common modern work...not at all bad, but entirely without any distinct character or excellence".

Postill

Robert Postill of York first appears on the scene in January 1866 for tuning and repairs to the value of £59/11/6d. What is more surprising is that he should then have been employed to undertake major rebuilding works. He was obviously respected, a worthy craftsman, but largely unknown to fame and not known to have been involved in any other project as prestigious as that at Durham Cathedral. One may wonder from the short-lived outcome of his efforts whether Postill bit off rather more than he could chew, or perhaps his work was simply overtaken by events.

Repairs and additions were ordered on the 16th June 1866. From September are numerous payments to the Railway Company for the carriage of "organ work" and later, "organ pipes" some "from London". By the 9th November the local newspaper is able to report that "The Cathedral organ is at present undergoing extensive alterations and repairs. The Swell is being increased and a Pedal organ added. It will be some time before work is completed".

Robert Postill was paid £465/10/- for the "Balance of the work at the Cathedral organ" on the 26th January 1867, but there is no surviving record of any earlier payment. In the normal way of such contracts the total cost of the work must have been at least twice the balance, ie. over £900. There was additional expense of carriage of materials and ancillary joinery and mason's work costing £170 and also a donation of £50 to Dr. Armes in acknowledgement of services rendered during the reconstruction.

A long, detailed and entertaining report of this last exercise with the 180 year old organ is provided in the *Durham Advertiser* of the 25th January 1867. Details of the repairs and changes are specified. The bellows and feeders were thoroughly renovated and a new Pedal bellows provided. The entire mechanism was overhauled - "the hundred and one things which form the component parts of that complicated whole, a large organ". A handsome new drawstop action [console] and a new set of German pedals of full range were made and the compass of the manuals extended and standardised; several short compass stops were made full compass. To the Great a Piccolo 2ft was added, and to the Swell six stops - Bourdon 16ft, Gamba 8ft, Clarionette Flute 8ft, Octave Quint 2²/₃, Super Octave 2ft and Mixture IV ranks - transforming that department from "by far the weakest" to "one of the largest and most effective Swells in the North of England". The new Pedal division provided both delicate, soft stops, yet could be "commanding, massive and grand". A stop list of the organ 1867 to 1873 is provided elsewhere in this book, with its earlier states for comparison.

Postill is lauded as having conquered the innumerable difficulties with which he had to contend, acting in the double capacity of conservator and reformer; "his courage and ability must redound to his reputation as an excellent and judicious organ builder ... placing the instrument amongst the first-class organs of England". "All the old beautiful toned pipes ... fine old stops" were retained. He "has our best congratulations for his admirable success in renovation and addition, eschewing that favourite inclination of organ builders, namely destruction".

Dr. Armes in a report on the remains in 1883 is quite scathing. Postill's work is described as "of such a sort that its amalgamation with other men's work would be an act which I could not possibly approve ... the Postill work should never find its way into an organ again"!

T.H. Collinson [the "organist's apprentice" 1871-75] much later in life - in an article published 60 years later - recalled the Postill rebuild:
"...Apprenticeship to the sound musician and contrapuntist, Dr. Armes of Durham brought me into touch with the Father Smith organ of the Cathedral, amended "up-to-date"(!) by one Postil [sic] of York. My fellow pupils shared with me the wonder felt for the Doctor's handiness and impetuosity in playing this instrument. If, as sometimes happened, the tumbler coupler, Swell to Great, got out of gear and caused trouble, he would accompany the choir with one hand, while undoing the front boards with the other, to push into place some erring sticker. His impetuosity shewed itself on the occasion of a rebellious stop-handle refusing to go "in", by his planting his back against the Choir organ panel behind the stool and booting the unfortunate stop in with the full thrust of his right leg. This was quite effective and the Principal humbly became dumb to order. The low pressure Diapasons of Father Smith were very mellow and soft, and were the admiration of many musicians visiting the Cathedral. A 16ft Trombone ... came out only on high days and holidays and the comment of an intelligent chorister on its appearance in Mozart's Glory, Honour was in the form of a question: 'Was the organ-case rattling today?' The lack of a 16ft stop on the Great organ seemed to be atoned for by the old fashioned ponderousness of Dr. Armes' playing; he was really great at "filling up" his harmonies, and was a Handelian player of the first water..."

The last record of work here by the York builder is a resolution of the 28th May 1870 "that Mr. Postill thoroughly clean the organ and do any necessary repairs". In February 1873 the Chapter Clerk was instructed to write to Postill to inform him that his engagement at the Cathedral Organ must terminate, as it was necessary that the temporary organ which would be placed for some time in the Cathedral must be under the control of its builders.

The restoration of the Cathedral was afoot and the Quire area was closed off and services transferred to the nave and crossing between April 1873 and October 1876. Collinson's *The Diary of an Organist's Apprentice at Durham Cathedral 1871-1875* tells how Dr. Armes and the Precentor, Thomas Rogers, helped by Collinson, took the pipes out of the old organ in May 1873. By Ascension Day, the 22nd May: "The organ is all away now. The pipes are in the library and the case, some in the treasury and some in the triforium, I think". And so the story of the Father Smith organ ends - or does it?

West view of the Father Smith organ on the screen: R. W. Billings, 1843

2
Dispersal

The pipes and parts of the organ dismantled in 1873 remained stored and unmentioned for several years. Chapter in November 1879, however, "agreed to present the Choir organ portion of the old Cathedral organ to the Castle Chapel" and two weeks later: "To authorise Dr. Armes to save all the pipes that can be saved of the Great and Swell portions ... to make a list of them and to stack them carefully". Armes's list is not now to be found, but appears to have formed the basis of later letters and reports which are extant, and comprise the best information available, with little remaining organ material as evidence.

The Castle Organ

The Choir division of the old organ was incorporated complete in 1880 into an organ for the Tunstall Chapel of University College, Durham. The Bishop 1859 chest and nine ranks (variously by Smith, Snetzler, Bishop and Postill - if as it seems there were no substitutions) were re-assembled and re-used as the Swell of the new instrument, built against the rear wall and roof of the chapel. Great and Pedal stops and all the workings of the organ were made new by Harrison & Harrison, then eight years established in Durham. Father Smith's Chaire case, with its decorated pipes - once so imposing above the Quire door - was re-used, resurrected on a gallery position at the west end of the Chapel, where it proudly perches to this day. In 1926 the instrument itself was completely rebuilt in the then current style, as a two manual with 9 speaking stops; more changes were made by transposing ranks when the organ was again restored in 1981. The organ has recently been restored without change, and the case woodwork and painted front pipes carefully cleaned, the splendour of its carving and decoration more fully revealed [illustrated p.29]. The pipework is a medley. Of old material, only the Father Smith Fifteenth 2ft survives, now as the Great 4ft, together with part of the Swell 4ft Flute (with tops remade and with wooden stoppers). Buckingham says that Snetzler inserted this rank on the Chaire in place of Smith's wooden Flute in 1765. It is curious therefore to find that the original parts of the pipes have Smith markings and typical mouths (though ears are removed) - indeed that Armes and others believed them Smith pipes. It could be that Snetzler remade these pipes, or that Buckingham was wrong in his attribution!

Dr. Armes's House organ

Thomas Harrison also built a small organ at Dr. Armes's house, 17 North Bailey, completed in July 1880. A letter from him seems to suggest building a two stop, two manual organ to Armes's wishes, costing £33. Armes would supply some pipes and parts - presumably out of the old Cathedral organ. The size envisaged does not however tie up with later recollections, for it seems to have had 4 stops on 1 manual, pipes enclosed in a Swell box, and coupled pedal. Certainly in a letter to the Chapter Clerk in 1903, Armes states that "...the pipes of the four stops which were once in the old Cathedral organ and which the Dean & Chapter kindly allowed me the use of in a small organ that I got Mr. Harrison to build for me, that I might not be deprived of the power of private practice by the coming of the new organ in 1876, are now restored to the Dean & Chapter's care in the new Song School".

As Armes records the four "borrowed" stops were:

  i) Stopped Diapason 8ft tone, wood, by Bernard Smith [Great]
  ii) Flute 4ft tone, wood, by Bernard Smith [Great]
  iii) Clarabella (TC) 8ft, [mostly] by Bishop 1844; Tenor octave by Postill [Great]
  iv) Bell Gamba (TC) 8ft, by some London maker to the order of Mr. Postill of York [Swell]

Dr. Armes's small organ was placed in the Song School in 1902, and its future there will be noted under that heading.

The remains

Armes by 1883 avers that in storage many of the larger metal pipes were "broken and sunk down by age, by ten years of lying down, and by the unhappy treatment they received in their removal from the Library to the Triforium (by whose order I was never able to find out)". At the same meeting [7th March 1903] as it thanked Dr. Armes for presenting his house organ for use in the new Song School, Chapter "agreed that the Dean see to the portions of the old Cathedral Organ stored in the Clerestory [sic] of the Cathedral". Two months later the Dean presented a Report, dated 14.5.1903, prepared "by the help of Dr. Armes". This indicates that "the smaller metal pipes have many of them suffered very badly. There is a heap of a hundred or more lying in a heap worthy to be used only as metal. On the other hand there are very many of the better metal and wooden pipes in excellent condition. They sound their note perfectly well. The large metal pipes which have been painted to stand in the front of the old organ are sadly knocked about. It would be a great pity not to make use, while life remains in them, of the fine and original parts of this organ".

Chapter agreed to "sanction the calling in of Mr. Harrison the organ-builder [whom in the Dean's words "Dr. Armes considers to be very capable and completely to be trusted"] to look through the remains of the old organ and give the Dean & Chapter a professional opinion as to whether they could hope to create a good Father Smith organ out of the ruins and what would be the cost of it with, and without, a case". This was the year when Harrison created a two manual organ at Auckland Castle Chapel, incorporating the case front and several ranks from the small "Father Smith" instrument there. The organ-builder's reply to Chapter, including the following stop list of a proposed two manual organ, is in both the Cathedral and the Harrison firm's records. There was enough old pipework available to form the nucleus of a good, useful and effective instrument. New ranks to each manual and a new Pedal section would be added to complete and balance the organ, which would be up-to-date in its mechanical arrangements, everything but the old pipes being newly made:

Great C/a³ - 58

1. Double Claribel Flute		16ft	wood, closed bass.
2. Open Diapason I	Smith	8ft	metal, part new
3. Open Diapason II	Smith	8ft	metal
4. Stopped Diapason	Smith	8ft	wood [ex house organ]
5. Octave	Smith	4ft	metal
6. Stopped Flute	Smith	4ft	metal + wood [ex house organ]
7. Octave Quint		2²/3ft	metal
8. Super Octave	Smith	2ft	metal

Swell C/a^3 - 58

1. Contra Gamba		16ft	metal, closed wood bass
2. Open Diapason	Jordan	8ft	metal
3. Lieblich Gedeckt		8ft	wood + metal
4. Salicional		8ft	metal
5. Octave	Jordan	4ft	metal
6. Flute a Cheminée	Jordan	4ft	metal
7. Oboe		8ft	metal
8. Contra Fagotto		16ft	metal } separate
9. Cornopean		8ft	metal } \wind pressure

Pedal C/f^1 - 30

1. Open Diapason	16ft	wood
2. Principal	8ft	18 by transmission
3. Bourdon	16ft	wood
4. Flute	8ft	18 by transmission

Couplers
Swell Octave, Great to Pedal, Swell to Pedal, Swell to Great

Tubular pneumatic action

3 combinations each to Great and Swell; Great to Pedal on/off
Radiating/concave pedal board, Willis type.
45 degree angle jambs, stop handles solid ivory, through ivory bushes.

Tuned to same pitch as large organ.
Cost £765, plus £109 for optional plain case.

Harrison & Harrison reported that, including the ranks from Dr. Armes's small organ, there were mainly five and possibly six stops of pipes by Father Smith and three stops by Jordan which were capable, with great care, of satisfactory restoration. This assessment generally conforms with a report by Dr. Armes to Chapter in 1883 in which he identifies this old pipework, the three short-compass Jordan ranks being Open and Stopt Diapasons and a Principal. It seems therefore in Arthur Harrison's scheme the 8ft chimneyed metal Stopt Diapason was to be transposed to a 4ft. However it is difficult to see how the proposed Swell 4ft Octave could have been a 1748 stop when the Swell division Jordan installed comprised only four 8ft stops - two flues and two reeds. It is now known that the Swell 4ft Principal (= Octave) was added by England in 1815, but the evidence of the pipes themselves cannot have been so clear in 1883 and 1903.

It seems from a letter that Dr. Armes thought the scheme ambitious, but Arthur Harrison justified it as "giving a small organ that would be of some use in the Cathedral ... nothing less could give satisfactory results". "No one is better able than yourself to assure the Chapter that the cost is moderate for the very best work, and nothing in the Cathedral should fall short of this". Harrison reported that the remainder of the material in the Triforium consisted chiefly of pipes of inferior quality by builders of later date and of worn out mechanism, which were of no great interest and of very little intrinsic value.

There is however no record of any subsequent discussion in Chapter. Six months later, in November 1903, Messrs Harrison & Harrison were asked to furnish a specification and estimate to put the main Cathedral organ into good order, so any ideas of building a small organ from the remains of the old organ sank without trace. Dean Kitchin writing to Arthur Harrison thought that the task of restoring the Willis organ might "make up for the disappointment over the old organ".

Today in the Cathedral only a few fragments of carved casework but no pipes remain stored in a corner of the south nave triforium. The old keyboards were until recently displayed in the Monks' Dormitory and the supporting screen and upper parts of the former West Front case stand to a reduced height in the gloom in the south nave aisle - reassembled in 1934, though with undecorated dummy pipes made from cardboard tubes! Nevertheless, the richness and detail of the carving on the case can be seen and some impression is given of its former grandeur - "so good and sound mad as anny is in the holl worrelt".

"….an elegant double case, grand and stately" from a print looking west by R.W.Billings, 1843

3
The Gray & Davison organ 1873-76

Chapter on the 11th January 1873 considered a report by the Precentor about the hire of an organ to be used during the further progress of the works in the Cathedral. It was agreed to hire a new organ to be built by Messrs Gray & Davison of London, for 3 years at £50 a year, the Dean & Chapter paying the cost of carriage and erection. The Precentor and Dr. Armes were authorised to see to the necessary arrangements. The Dean & Chapter did not pledge themselves to engage the services of Messrs Gray & Davison for any work which might later be required for the existing organ.

The organ seems to have been installed to the side of the crossing in one of the transepts; which is not certain. It was new-built for the purpose and was valued by the firm at £500. The builder's books [in the British Organ Archive] provide these details:

Great (58)		**Swell** (58)		**Pedal** (30)
1. Contra Gamba	16	1. Lieblich Bourdon	16	1. Grand Open Diapason 16
2. Open Diapason	8	2. Spitzflote	8	2. Grand Bourdon 16
3. Keraulophon (gr.b)	8	3. Lieblich Gedackt	8	
4. Clarionet Flute with		4. Viol d'Amour (gr.b)	8	
St.D.Bass	8	5. Octave	4	
5. Octave	4	6. Sifflote	2	4 composition pedals to Great
6. Flute	4	7.Oboe	8	2 composition pedals to Swell
7. Twelfth	2²/3	8. Clarion	4	
8. Fifteenth	2			Great Manual to Pedals
9. Mixture	II			Swell Manual to Pedals
10.Trumpet	8			Swell to Great Manual

Front of deal, stained and varnished, and decorated pipes. 12ft wide, "simple height and depth".

There is a first-hand if brief record of the preliminaries to and erection of this organ in T.H.Collinson's Diary. In February [1873] two pipes from the old organ were taken to the railway station for transport to the organ builder, who presumably needed them for scaling and comparision. Erection of the new organ commenced on the 5th April, tuning was in hand by the 16th and the instrument was available and used for rehearsal on the 19th. By the 24th, Collinson thought "the new organ is very sweet, has a good deal of power. Some of the reeds were out of tune tonight".

This temporary organ was removed in October 1876, soon after the official opening of the new Willis organ in the restored Quire. Chapter Minutes record a dispute with the organ builders about the not insubstantial costs of removal from the Cathedral and carriage to its new home in St. Paul's, Newport Road, Middlesbrough. There was a disagreement over interpretation of wording in the firm's original letter to Dr. Armes and to resolve the matter, John Stainer - the organist of St. Paul's Cathedral - was brought in to arbitrate, seemingly finding in the Chapter's favour.

In Middlesbrough it was "reconstructed" for £518 by Norman & Beard of Norwich and London in 1911, retaining all the 1873 pipework and structure, but providing a third manual, some new stops, new console and tubular pneumatic action - in which condition it continued with little further alteration up to the church's closure in 1964. Fortunately then the organ was transferred to the west gallery of St. Peter's, Redcar, where it remains. Though cloaked in a modernist wooden slatted case hiding the original of three flats, the large-scale structure, Great and Swell chests and box, winding (G&D weights) and virtually all the 1873 pipework except the Swell 16ft survive as a forgotten reminder from the Cathedral's past.

The Smith Chaire case, now in University College Chapel [© C. Ladogorski]

4
The Father Willis organ

When Philip Armes came to Durham Cathedral as Organist in 1862, he must surely have been appalled at the sad hotch-potch of an organ which was all that remained of Father Smith's noble instrument of 1685/86. Armes's career had already been outstanding; he had achieved spectacular success as a Chorister of Rochester Cathedral, and by the time of his appointment to Durham at the age of 26 he had already been Organist of Chichester Cathedral for a year. He was in fact one of the leading organists of his generation - a generation which had seen enormous advances in the field of organ design and construction, and which would have expected something considerably larger and more up-to-date in the way of an organ in a cathedral of Durham's pre-eminence.

So it is no surprise that as part of George Gilbert Scott's re-ordering of the Quire which took place between 1873 and 1876, the Dean and Chapter decided to purchase a new instrument which would be worthy of its situation. Nor is it surprising that the choice of builder should have been Henry Willis. The leading organ-builder of his day - and arguably the greatest English organ-builder since Father Smith - he was responsible for building or rebuilding organs in eighteen British cathedrals during his lifetime. His father, a builder, was himself a musician; from him Henry inherited both a love of music and an understanding of structural theory, allied to supreme craftsmanship. These qualities, together with his acquired understanding of the properties of metal and of pipe design and his considerable technique as a performer, were enough to ensure Willis's success as an organ-builder; his genius as a voicer and his vision of what an organ should be marked him off as second to none. Every one of his organs, from the smallest to the largest, bears the unmistakable stamp of the skill of Father Willis's firm; the title 'Father', only previously given to Father Smith, was given to him as a mark of respect at the end of his life. His organs are characterised especially by the extreme clarity and brilliance of their flue-work, and by the brightness and sonority of their reeds, which have a truly orchestral quality.

Father Willis's organ was completed in March 1877. It was divided on either side of the Quire in the second bay east of the crossing. The Great was on the south side with the Solo close above it, as were the console and some of the Pedal; the Choir and the remainder of the Pedal were on the North side with the Swell above. The action was tubular pneumatic throughout; blowing was by three hydraulic engines. The organ cost £3,150.

On the day of the organ's opening (18 October 1876, the feast of St Luke) only nine stops on the Great and the Great to Pedal coupler were in use. Father Willis is reported as having screwed on the stop-knobs ten minutes before the first choral service. It must be said that this sort of thing was not a unique occurrence!

It is impossible at this distance in time to know how the Durham organ sounded. The instrument in Salisbury Cathedral, built by Willis the same year, has survived more intact, and is justly renowned as being of unusual splendour and excellence. If Durham's was of anything like the same quality, it must have been magnificent indeed. Contemporary reports are few, though.

What is clear is that from a fairly early stage the organ suffered mechanical problems. This may seem strange in view of what has been said about Willis's workmanship; undoubtedly one major factor was the Cathedral's heating system, whose stoves caused fumes to be spread through the building and into the organ, where they played havoc with the pipework and action. The hydraulic blowing system (whose internal layout had to be improved early on in order to maintain constant pressure) had soon been discarded in favour of gas blowing, but this in turn caused unconsumed gas to be blown through the instrument - and, like the hydraulic system, it was incapable of producing enough wind to power the full organ. The construction of tubular pneumatic action through a distance of seventy feet under the floor of the Quire - to transmit the player's actions to that part of the organ on the other side - was likewise stretching the limits of the technology of the time, and the internal layout of the organ, especially the cramped position of the Solo above the Great (some of whose pipes actually came into contact with the Solo chests) left much to be desired. But it is easy to criticise the builder; it must also be said that over a period of nearly thirty years little money was spent on any serious maintenance apart from the remaking of the bellows, and after that amount of daily use it was not surprising that the organ was in need of more fundamental repair, given the size and complexity of its mechanism and the enormous number of moving parts. In fact, by 1903 it had become partly unplayable. Philip Armes, in a letter to the Dean and Chapter written on 3 November, speaks of the Swell having been entirely out of action for some time past, and of notes on the Choir and Pedal which were permanently silent.

[For more detail about the original Willis organ see the webpage http://www.duresme.org.uk/CATH/willis.htm]

5
Harrison & Harrison re-buildings

During the last decade of the century Henry Willis had been approached with a view to repair and restoration, but nothing had actually been done. By the time of Dr. Armes's letter to the Chapter, Father Willis was dead. The family firm might well have been asked to undertake restoration, and it was clearly Armes's wish that it should do so. But Dean Kitchin had other ideas, and on 21 November 1903 Chapter asked the local firm of Harrison & Harrison to make a report. Dr Armes's protest was over-ruled; he seems, in fact, to have been quickly won round. Arthur Harrison produced the report on 4 December and the firm was instructed to proceed with the work, at an estimated maximum cost of £1,400.

The firm of Harrison & Harrison was at this time becoming well established. Since Thomas Harrison had moved his Works from Rochdale to Durham in 1872, where the firm set up as Harrison & Harrison, many contracts had come its way, some of them large and prestigious. But the firm had never had the opportunity to build or rebuild an English cathedral organ; now, here was a chance, right on the doorstep. The firm's report was thorough, and the recommendations were, briefly, to install new improved tubular pneumatic action throughout; to add thumb-pistons, combination couplers and two further manual couplers; to clean and overhaul the entire instrument, regulate the pipe-work and fit tuning slides; to alter the position of certain Pedal stops, and fit beards to the lower octave of the Swell Viol d'Amour, and, finally, to enclose the Choir organ in a swell-box.

Such a scheme was not unreasonable, given the circumstances. However, as the work progressed, ideas changed considerably. To cut a long story short, much of the organ was re-voiced, several extra stops were prepared for in anticipation of an enhanced tonal scheme, electro-pneumatic action was installed to the north side of the organ, and the Solo organ was moved (at an extra cost of £115) to the first bay east of the crossing on the south side - a wise move which relieved much overcrowding and allowed the Great to be heard to better effect - all this in addition to the work mentioned above. At the same time, the doors at the back of the case on the south side were installed, replacing a calico covering which had done little to protect that side of the organ from the sun's rays. There was evidently every expectation that the stops prepared for to complete the Harrison scheme would be installed within the next few years. Last but not least, electric blowing and new feeder bellows were installed, at a cost of £669/5/0d.

No new ranks were actually inserted at this stage. Nevertheless, the re-voicing which took place meant that this rebuild of 1905 saw probably the most drastic change the organ has ever undergone. The question must inevitably be asked why a fine instrument by such an eminent builder should need alteration; indeed it is heartbreaking that so few of Father Willis's large instruments have survived unaltered. The answer has to be that the fashion of the time dictated such changes. Willis's sparkling choruses and unrestrainedly colourful reeds did not appeal to a generation which expected more massive foundation tone and high-pressure, tromba-like reeds. One is tempted to suggest that the Choir and Solo had limitations as Willis left them, but it is always dangerous to judge from appearances on paper. One could say the same say of the Swell at St George, Gateshead, or of the

Choir at Blenheim Palace, for instance, but in each case the reality is utterly convincing. The fact that there was only a very small number of soft accompanimental stops under expression must have been trying - only the Swell was enclosed - and the absence of thumb pistons is odd, not least since Willis had fitted them as early as 1851 to the organ he built for the Great Exhibition at Crystal Palace. Arthur Harrison's report of 1903 to the Dean and Chapter, which criticises the small number of composition pedals, advises the addition of 'an adequate number of thumb pistons and combination pedals', made possible with the improved action.

Reaction to the re-build was mixed, though largely appreciative. Thomas Collinson, who had been an articled pupil of Philip Armes at the time the organ was built, and who was by now the first Organist of St Mary's Episcopal Cathedral, Edinburgh, wrote:

"Alas, that that glorious organ as completed by Father Willis was only allowed to remain undisturbed for some thirty years, when it was not only fitted with newer action and console, but was re-voiced! The Willis Tuba of 22 inches wind had timbre, almost vocal in its beauty – but now . . ."

The eulogy by James Wedgwood printed in the Musical Opinion for December 1905 was probably more in keeping with the age; after reviewing the whole organ, he says:

"I need not multiply instances. I can pay a high compliment to Messrs Harrison by saying that it is now an organ with all the unrivalled boldness and splendour of Willis's work but with the faults of Willis - and they were by no means insignificant - reduced to a minimum."

In fact, while one cannot but regret that Father Willis's handiwork should have needed to be touched, one can only rejoice at the quality of the work that was done. Arthur Harrison was to become known as the finest voicer of his generation, and the firm's craftsmanship was evident at every level, tonal and mechanical. If the organ had been fine before, it was no less fine now; in a different way, but still with supreme and consistent quality.

Arthur Harrison's final aims in this rebuild were summed up in his own article in the brochure for the organ's re-opening in July 1905:

"The tonal scheme has been re-modelled with the view of supplementing the foundation tone and giving to each department a well-balanced harmonic structure of its own, but the superb brilliancy of tone which was the chief characteristic of this organ, as of all the late Henry Willis's larger work, has been carefully retained. . . ."

[An extended article about the Harrisons' approach and the rebuilding may be found in an article: "Arthur Harrison, R.Meyrick Roberts, George Dixon, and the remodelling of Durham cathedral organ in 1904/5", in the British Institute of Organ Studies' Journal 18 (1994)].

By all accounts the rebuilt organ seems to have given excellent service; the mechanical problems and the shortage of wind were at last overcome, and the instrument behaved with the reliability which has always been a hallmark of Harrison organs. But the work had cost considerably more than the £1400 budgeted. Even then, it is difficult to see how the firm made any profit, so much greater was the amount of work done than had been bargained for. Time went by with no sign of the additional stops being provided.

Armes had resigned to retirement in 1907. It was not until the late 1920s that serious plans were made to complete the tonal scheme. By the time work was started, Durham had a new Dean - Cyril Alington, a man of energy and vision - and a new Organist, John Dykes Bower, in succession to Arnold Culley, who had for many years combined this duty with that of Precentor. Dykes Bower was probably the leading organist of his generation. He had become Organist of Truro Cathedral at the age of 21; three years later, he went as Organist to New College, Oxford, whence he came to Durham in 1933. During his short time at Durham he took his Doctorate; but in 1936 he was appointed to St Paul's Cathedral. Following his retirement, he was knighted on New Year's Day 1968. His brother, the eminent architect Stephen Dykes Bower, drew up a scheme with a drawing for restoring the Durham organ to a screen position. Whatever the merits or demerits of such a scheme from a wider point of view, one must say that musically it would have been very exciting. But it was not to be.

It has often been commented that the enlargements of 1935 tallied remarkably closely with the scheme put forward thirty years before. To some extent this was deliberately so; the Pedal gained two heavy reeds and (by extension) a lighter Open Wood. But in addition the large Open Wood was carried up to 8 ft and 4 ft pitches, and two new Solo basses were made available also on the Pedal. The Choir gained further foundation tone and a small Mixture, as envisaged. The Solo was at last enclosed, and moved up into the triforium on the north side, high above the Swell organ; from its elevated position it does speak clearly into the whole building. Here Arthur Harrison's mature voicing skills found full expression; the family of strings (seven ranks), the Cor Anglais and the French Horn were all truly magnificent examples. The flutes and other soft reeds, somewhat re-voiced, also gained much from being put under expression. The Orchestral Tuba, a 'bridge' between the Great reeds and the massive Solo Tubas, was a more useful addition than the planned Tromba would have been; it would have been nice to have had the 16 ft Trombone, though!

It was on the Great that changing ideas made themselves most felt. The 1905 scheme had provided, rather unnecessarily one feels, for two further flutes in addition to the three at 8ft or 4ft which were already there. There was also, conceived in 1935 itself, a scheme to replace the Gamba with a 32 ft Quintaton to tenor C; mercifully this was not pursued. Instead, the Diapason tone was supplemented with a new small Open Diapason to bridge the gap between the flutes and the (fairly big) second Open; a new 4 ft Principal was added to match. A new large Open, leathered, somewhat outside the chorus but adding solid foundation tone, completed the line-up of four Open Diapasons. This sounds a lavish number, but it cannot be said that any one of the four is really a luxury. The original two were enough to support the chorus, but the gravitas needed in much early twentieth-century English music is not there, and the smaller of the original Opens is simply too loud for much accompanimental work. That said, the 1935 additions do not have the freshness or the singing quality of the original Open Diapasons or the Double, to any of which on their own one can happily listen for an extended period.

Finally, the unenclosed Tubas were moved to a new position in the first bay east of the crossing on the north side, where they were joined by the new Pedal Ophicleides. Since 1970 these four stops have been known as the Bombarde division.

Once again, the accessories were up-dated; in particular, the list of couplers was made both conventional and complete. The sub- and super-octave coupling on the Swell which the Willis Swell to Great couplers made available had been removed in 1905, never to return; given the size of the Swell, their use must have been devastating in effect.

The organ could now at last claim to be a complete and up-to-date four-manual, large enough to cope with the biggest occasions, and with a wealth of soft, enclosed, accompanimental stops. The quality of the work was supreme throughout - and here one is speaking not only with the evidence of personal recollections of those who still remember it from that time, but from experience, for virtually the whole scheme was left intact in the 1970 rebuild.

Upon Dr. Dykes Bower's departure in 1936, Conrad Eden was appointed Organist. During the next thirty-eight years his name became synonymous with the Durham organ; his intimate knowledge of it and his outstanding playing made him a legend in his own lifetime. It was fitting that towards the end of his time at Durham the organ should be cleaned and repaired; in particular, the action - which again was becoming elderly and noisy - was replaced by electro-pneumatic action throughout. This work was carried out under the leadership of Cuthbert Harrison, the third generation of the family in organ-building.

Once again, fashions had changed, and (largely under the influence of the Organ Reform Movement, still only partly understood in this country at the time) an ideal organ of this size was expected to possess rather more in the way of upper-work and mutations. More importantly, the increasing use of the Nave for services made it necessary to explore ways in which the sound of the organ could be better projected westward. The decision was therefore taken to add a Positive division, playable on the Choir keys but transferable to other keyboards. It was installed with minimum "casework" on top of the Choir box moved to the first bay east of the crossing on the south side - the position where the Solo had been from 1905 to 1935. The original suggestions for a stop-list were somewhat conservative, with basically a straight Diapason chorus and two chorus reeds, 8ft and 4ft; ideas developed, however, to culminate in the unusual but versatile adopted scheme. Particularly useful are the two separate Cornet combinations - one at 8ft pitch and one at 4ft - and the light, free-speaking 16ft Dulzian. The possibilities of the department are increased by the fact that, when transferred to the Solo, the Solo sub- and super-octave couplers affect it, so that it can be employed at different pitches in relation to the rest of the organ.

It is a pity that the four manual divisions and pedal are no longer within the one bay, and that the Swell and Choir are now so far apart, but the new layout gives more room for the pipes to speak out properly. The Choir and the Positive also gain by being close together. For the rest, the pipework was left much as it had been, except that the Great Mixture was remade to a new composition (with the seventeenth omitted), and a new higher mixture, the Scharf, added. The Choir gained a Nazard and Tierce, very useful ranks, quite different in style from the mutations on the Positive. The Open Diapason and Viola da Gamba of 1935 were dispensed with - the only ranks ever to have left the organ (though quite a few other stops, especially the Great and Pedal Mixtures, have at different stages been altered in almost everything but name). The loss of the Viola was largely made up by the exchange of the Salicional with the Viole d'Amour, giving the Choir a more sizeable string stop, and reuniting the Salicional with the Vox Angelica, now on the Swell. This was evidently a last-minute decision; the official photographs of the console, taken in the works, show the Salicional on the Choir and the Viole d'Amour on the Swell. One has to say, though, that the Choir Open Diapason is missed. New ranks - some using discarded Choir pipework - were added to the Pedal. The 16 ft Trombone was extended downwards most successfully by the addition of twelve pipes to form a 32 ft octave. Given the overpowering scale of the 32 ft Ophicleide, it is very useful to have a smaller 32 ft reed for those occasions when ff, as opposed to fff, is what is required!

Finally, the console was entirely rebuilt with new keyboards and a slightly unusual design, to the specification of Conrad Eden. This included a frighteningly original layout of the pedal pistons, replaced by a more straightforward design in 1982. That apart, the console design is characterised by its extreme ease of handling, comfort and reliability. Although the organ is very large, it is not difficult to manage. The Willis keyboards, altered by Harrison & Harrison but discarded in 1970, were on view in the Monks' Dormitory until recent years, but are now conserved in storage.

It will be noticed from the specifications that every one of the 1876 ranks has survived in at least vestigial form. But it must at the same time be stressed that the character of the instrument changed with extensive re-voicing in 1905, and to a lesser extent in 1935. With the few exceptions noted above, no re-voicing took place in 1970. Even the Great Gamba has survived several attempts at its suppression. It is a useful rank in its own right, despite being one of no fewer than seven 8 ft flues in this division.

It is occasionally commented that some of the 1970 upperwork stands out (in aural terms) from the rest of the organ. To an extent this comment is justified, though the passage of time and a certain amount of regulation has in some degree, ameliorated this; still, it is true that one has to pick and choose one's registration perhaps more selectively than one does with the older parts of the organ. What can be said is that the new work has added useful voices to the organ which were not present before, without in any way compromising the integrity of the 1935 scheme; there is still a very complete underlying four manual and pedal scheme without the 1970 work. But the new work undoubtedly helps the organ's sound output to travel down the building - vital on the many occasions when the Nave is full of people singing. To suggest that one single organ should be capable of meeting every need in a building of this size and of these acoustic problems would be wishful thinking; compared with many of the organs in England's larger cathedrals, though, Durham's goes a long way towards fulfilling this aim. And probably not a week goes by but every stop in the organ is used at some time.

Over many years the Durham organ has attracted an enviable reputation - one might almost say mystique - all its own. Laurence Elvin, in "The Harrison Story", writes:

"It is a great mistake to describe any one Cathedral organ as the finest of them all; there are a number of outstanding instruments each with their own marked individuality, yet I would express the opinion that no other organ, apart from Willis's masterpiece at St Paul's Cathedral, provides me with quite the same aural experience as that at Durham Cathedral . . . Superb voicing, excellent acoustics and an incomparable setting all contribute to make it one of the great treasures of the English speaking world."

What is the secret of this instrument that marks it out so specially in the minds of so many who have heard it or played it?

A major factor must of course be the incomparable nature of the building, the grandeur of its setting, and the ever-present sense of history and of holiness. The acoustics of the building have much to do with it too - but that is axiomatic, for an organ, of all musical instruments, is most particularly conceived in terms of a specific acoustic and space. But it is the consistent quality of the work, its voicing, its colour, and its supreme blend, which makes for a satisfying effect; that and the great comprehensiveness of the scheme. Equally important, too, is the ability of all the ranks to speak freely into the building; for the effect of even the best organ is ruined if the internal layout is cramped. From many parts of the building, but particularly from the eastern part of the Quire, the organ can be heard to sing naturally and freely. The quality of the action and the player's position within the organ (fortunately left unchanged) ensure contact and rapport with the instrument - obviously not to the same extent as a mechanical action would allow, but such a thing would be out of the question in such an organ as this with the distance and the high wind-pressures involved. Quite simply, the player feels part of the instrument. Successive re-buildings have changed the quality of the organ, to the extent that it is unreal to pretend that there is any longer much trace of Father Willis's work; but the instrument has not suffered, as have so many, in the course of these changes. It is different, but equally valid. Again, one can only give thanks for the quality of Arthur Harrison's work.

That the organ continues to give such magnificent service and to contribute so nobly to the music of the Cathedral, bringing pleasure and inspiration to countless numbers of people, is overwhelmingly due to the presence of a world-famous firm of organ builders in this small northern city. Since 1905 Harrison & Harrison has spared no pains to ensure that this organ, justly the source of so much pride, is kept in first-class condition. The fact that the firm should have resisted the bright lights of the metropolis and stayed true to its northern origins has done much for the community and has put Durham firmly on the organ map of the world. No record of the organ's history would be complete without a tribute to the firm's dedication and workmanship.

Such an enormous piece of equipment inevitably needs maintenance; to tune the organ all through requires four working days. This is done annually, in addition to the monthly one-day tunings. Gone are the days when the cathedral organist tuned the reeds himself each week, as Philip Armes did! That in itself is a measure of the commitment of the Chapter to its upkeep. Long may this noble instrument continue to sound to the glory of God and to the comfort, healing and inspiration of those who hear it.

The south side front of the organ from the north Quire triforium [© C.R.A.Davies]

6
The organ cases

An organ should be as pleasing to the eye as to the ear, and its case is likely to be one of the largest and most imposing of church furnishings. Its purpose is not only decorative, but with traditional wooden cases, though the front is filled with display pipes, the structure and enclosure project and enhance the sound, as well as protecting the organ's internal workings.

At Durham Cathedral until 1847 the organ occupied a prominent position on the Quire screen. In monastic times, the screen with organ, together with the Jesus altar at the head of the nave, formed a solid barrier to the monastic sanctum. The finest of the organs, with gilded doors and carving, stood on the screen, facing east; we have to try to picture its appearance from the description in the *Rites of Durham* quoted earlier (p.8).

There is no known drawing or description of the organ built at Durham by Thomas Dallam in 1621, though we may take as some indication of the likely style and appearance the handful of pre-Commonwealth cases which survive in Britain, as well as other Dallam cases made during his son Robert's enforced stay in Brittany. The form of front using a curved cornice rising from a central low to high side towers was a favourite of the family. These cases provide a strong sense of perspective, even opportunities for *trompe l'oeil* decoration. Was it this 'swept' style, with as much a horizontal as vertical emphasis, like those Dallam provided at St George's Chapel, Windsor, and still to be seen at King's College, Cambridge, that was also employed at Durham? Or perhaps at Durham Dallam used a more vertical style with three tall towers, the largest in the centre, as provided by son Robert at York Minster in 1634? Unless or until a description comes to light, we do not know.

Nor is there any description of George Dallam's Restoration instrument of 1662, except that an Inventory refers to two sets of 'armes carved in wood set on ye loft organ'. With Father Smith's organ, however, comes certainty. The 1683 Agreement tells that the organ was to be provided

> ". . . with a Case of good sound and substantiall Oak wood according to a draught or modell of an organ in parchment ... [though this sketch has not survived]. [The] great Organ shall have a back front towards the body or west end of the Church which shall be in all things and respects like to the fore front both in pipes and carving ... [and] ... the pipes of the two fronts of the ... great Organ and the front pipes of the ... Chair [Choir] Organ are to be painted and guilt according to the best way and mode of painting & guilding of Organs."

The Chapter expected and got an elegant double case, grand and stately. Buckingham provides some dimensions:

Great Case of Oak:	27ft 9in. high, 18ft 6in. wide, 4ft 8in. deep
Choir Case of Oak:	9ft 0in. high, 9ft wide, 3ft deep.
	10ft 6in. high, from under the Truss & Architrave.

Sir John Sutton thought that:

"The cases which were built by Schmidt, in the latter part of the 17th century, are far better than any thing that has been built since, for although the detail is not ecclesiastical, still the old form is kept up ... the carved work is bold ... with large angels heads, and ... with the assistance of a hundred and sixty years, they look really venerable, especially when they have diapered pipes, which is the case in the Durham Cathedral organ."

Writing in 1847 (what irony, given its removal from the screen that year!), he recommended that these old cases should be allowed to remain because they provided a good example in an age of bad taste, and 'because nothing half so good can be procured at present'.

Illustrations in this booklet show what an imposing sight it was on the seventeenth century wooden screen dividing Quire from Nave - the main cases each a four tower 'baroque', but well proportioned composition, with the intervening flats horizontally divided, and the subsidiary Chaire case generally matching but with three towers, the tallest tower(s) being central. The towers stand on carved heads or leaf brackets, and the side overhang is supported by a scroll bracket. On top are huge mitres and Bishop Crewe's coat of arms. There is extensive carving in panels and friezes, in the pediment and pipe shades, which is boldly executed, to be viewed from below or at a distance. The pipes were richly decorated with scroll-work, cherubs, and heraldic devices. In Smith's own words: 'for carving and painting I have been too curious ... so good as could bee ... don for the honnor of Mr Lord and the Dean and Chapter'.

The circumstances of the organ with its cases being relegated to floor level on the north side of the Quire, and the whole effect spoilt, have already been described. The fate of the cases following the demise of the old organ in 1873 is not entirely calamitous - the Chair case with its decorated pipes lives on in the Castle (see the illustration on p. 29), and parts of the west front of the main case are reconstructed in the Cathedral - but the integrity of Smith's imposing creation in that focal position on the Quire screen has been forever lost.

Father Willis's organ, divided on both north and south sides in the second bay of the Quire, does not have cases in the proper sense. Willis 'cases' generally are not architectural; frankly they are a convenient repository for the large metal pipes, though at Durham the supporting structure and pipes were brightly and magnificently decorated by some of the best church artists of the day. Willis's collaboration with Sir George Gilbert Scott, the architect employed in the restoration of the Quire at Durham, here (as also at Salisbury and Hereford) resulted in what has been called `canister casework'.

The late Michael Gillingham, connoisseur of English organ cases, has commented:

"The Victorian pipe-fronts at Durham, decorated by Clayton and Bell in 1876 under the direction of C. Hodgson Fowler (architect to the Dean and Chapter) are outstanding examples of their kind, a purely Victorian invention to adorn a 'caseless' organ. Only the fronts at Eton College Chapel and St Michael, Tenbury can show anything quite comparable, but Eton is within a case and not intended to be seen initially from the side as are the Durham fronts; Tenbury is a single front. The Durham pipes are decorated in a noticeably restricted range of colours (black and red on gold) with bold horizontal treatment on the feet and angels playing instruments on the pipes of the three 'towers' of each front, above the delicate supporting ironwork. The ground-pattern is restrained; the whole effect is like that of a rich carpet. The panels of the coving were decorated later with musician angels, texts, and stars. The great success of the whole scheme is the way in which it blends with the architecture and achieves richness without ostentation."

The local newspaper after the opening in 1876 offers a more prosaic description:

"The two cases are of richly carved oak, each forming a cove arching over the canopies of the stalls and carried below on oak piers and arches. Above and around those coves are very richly and beautifully carved cornices, the design being composed of intersecting foliage, with birds and grotesque animals in the different openings of the twining branches. On these cornices stand the front pipes of the organ, magnificent tubes of metal of great size, all richly decorated . . . held in position by a band of ornamental ironwork. The oak work to the cases is by Mr. J. Roddis of Birmingham ..."

These fronts remain a distinguished statement of their time and of considerable interest in their own right [North front illustration p.52].

7
Other organs

Three small organs are reported at different times in **the Song School**.

Of the first very little is known. The Chapter Minutes of the 24th September 1711 instruct "That the small organ at Newcastle be bought for the use of the Song Schole". The Audit Book gives the cost - £12, and shows that two guineas was spent "mending the little organ" in 1727/8, and 15/- "Removing the Song School organ" in 1737/8.

Then, in November 1820, Chapter "Agreed that there be an Organ got for the Song School" and the surviving Notebook of A. Buckingham, the organ-builder at that time looking after the Cathedral's organs, gives us details:

Durham Cathedral Singing School
An organ with one set of Keys from GG long octaves to F in Alt with an octave of Pedals and a Piano movement.

Open Diapason from g	47 [pipes]
Stop Diapason bafs and treble	58
Dulciana treble from m/c	30
Principal	58
Fifteenth	58
	251

NB. The Open Diapason bafs is communicated to the Principal which gives a very fine effect with the Diapasons. The St. Diapason treble is metal.

In a Mahogany case with gilt front 9ft 8in high, 5ft 6in wide, and 2ft 11in deep.
Made by James Davies [actually Davis] of London and a very fine organ it is.
Sent from London and erected in the Song School August 1821 by A. Buckingham.

Chapter records show that this organ cost £120/9/-, including carriage.

The organ is mentioned fifty years after its acquisition in T. H. Collinson's Diary, when he was apprenticed to Dr. Armes. It seems the apprentices were able to use this small organ for practice, but seemingly paid for the privilege. Collinson's youthful view thought it "a very small weak instrument with only five stops and German pedals". The Diary informs us in August 1873 that "the old organ pedals [ie. from the dismantled Cathedral organ] are on the Song-school organ now". Repairs undertaken in 1880 apparently made use of the Postill 2ft wooden Piccolo from the dismantled Cathedral organ.

Since this book was first written, the subsequent history of the former Song School organ has been discovered. When the Song School moved in 1898, the organ seems to have been disposed of by the Cathedral, to re-appear at the Methodist Church in Congleton, Cheshire where it served, with some alteration, for some 80 years. In the 1980s it was moved to St. Barnabas, Wavertree, Liverpool, and then, after a few years in storage with an organ-builder, was installed at St. Pedrog, Llanbedrog, on the Lleyn Peninsula, North Wales, where it survives. A modern plate on the organ commemorating the donor also indicates that the organ was built in 1821 for Durham Cathedral. Photographs show a free-standing cabinet organ with fine gothick style mahogany casework, if with cosmetic changes.

Details of **Dr. Armes' house organ** have already been given. As well as clarifying which stops were "borrowed" from the Chapter, in his letter presenting the organ, Armes continues:-
"The rest of the organ now in the Song School - extra pipes, mechanism, case, manuals (these all by Harrison) and Pedals (these by Willis & Sons) - I very respectfully ask the Dean and Chapter to accept ... and that no word be said about the cost of removal please. The instrument is now in a perfectly clean state and in excellent working order...".

Later Harrison & Harrison "loaned" a new Pedal board - a duplicate of the one then going into the Cathedral organ. The firm kept the old board for the "purpose of illustration".

The organ stood to the right of the stairs leading into the present Song School over the Slype, and is recalled to this day, unflatteringly, by pupils of Armes's successor as Organist, A. D. Culley, who were given lessons on it. It was not apparently used for practices with the choir. On this evidence it is clear the organ remained in some use in the Song School until after 1927, though by 1936 it is recorded as having been dismantled and consigned to store. An amateur rebuilding attempt by staff and pupils of the Chorister School in 1953/4 failed, and it is reported that by 1974 there were no pipes left, only a set of bellows, a sound-board, the wreckage of the pedal board and a few trackers, since disposed of.

The **Laus Deo organ,** a continuo instrument on wheels, was built in 2004 by Lammermuir Pipe Organs, the firm's Opus 45. It was commissioned by the Cathedral Choir Association with the aid of a generous donation from Dr. David Boardman. The case of oak woodwork, stained to match the old choir stalls, has two towers and gilded front pipes. The four stops comprise: Stopped Diapason [wood] 8, Principal [partly in the case] 4, Nason Flute [wood] 4, and Fifteenth [wood] 2.

Appendix 1 : Father Smith's contract

Several contracts between Smith and his clients have been preserved. The Durham one is a typical and interesting example. It was first transcribed and printed in Sir John Sutton's *Short Account of Organs* [1847].

A.D. 1683.

Articles of agreement covenanted, concluded, and agreed upon the eighteenth day of August in the five and thirtieth year of the reign of our Sovereign Lord Charles the Second by the grace of God King of England, Scotland, France and Ireland, Defender of the faith. Between the Rt. Honble John Sudbury doctor of divinity, Dean and the Chapter of Durham of the Cathedral Church of Christ and blessed Mary the virgin of the one part and Bernard Smith of the city of London Organ maker of the other part as followeth.

Imprimis. It is agreed by and between the sd parties and the sd Bernard Smith for himself, [h]is Executors, and administrators, doth hereby covenant, promise, and agree to and with the sd Dean and Chapter and their successors by these presents that he the sd Bernard Smith for and in consideration of the severall sums of money hereinafter mentioned shall and will before the first day of May which will be in the year of our Lord one thousand six hundred and eighty five at his own proper cost and charges make and fitt up in the Organ loft of the sd Cathedral Church of Durham a good, perfect, laudable, and harmonious great Organ and Chair Organ with a Case of good sound and substantiall Oak wood according to a draught or modell of an organ in parchment whereon or whereunto all the sd partys have subscribed their names at or before the time of sealing and delivering of these presents.

Item it is agreed by and between the sd partys that the sd Bernard Smith shall make in the sd great organ these seventeen stops, viz., Two open diapasons of Mittall containing one hundred and eight pipes. A stop diapason of wood containing fifty four pipes. A principall of Mittall containing fifty four pipes. A cornet of Mittall containing nynety six pipes. A quinta of Mittall containing fifty four pipes. A super Octave of Mittall containing fifty four pipes. A Holfluit of wood containing fifty four pipes. A block flute of Mittall containing fifty four pipes. A small Quint of Mittall containing fifty four pipes. A mixture of three ranks of pipes of Mittall containing one hundred and sixty two pipes. A trumpet of Mittall containing fifty four pipes. And in the Chair organ five stops, viz., A principal of Mittall in the front containing fifty four pipes. A stop diapason of wood containing fifty four pipes. A voice Humand of Mittall containing fifty four pipes. A holfluit of wood containing fifty four pipes. And a super octave of Mittall containing fifty four pipes.

Item it is agreed by and between these parties that the sd great Organ shall have a back front towards the body or west end of the Church which shall be in all things and respects like to the fore front both in pipes and carving. And all the pipes belonging to the two diapason stops shall speak at will in the sd back front as in the fore.

Item in consideration of which work by the sd Bernard Smith to be done and formed in the manner and form aforesaid the sd Dean & Chapter for themselves and their successors do covenant and grant to and with the sd Bernard Smith his Executors and administrators by these presents in manner and form following that is to say that the sd Dean and Chapter shall and will well and truly pay or cause to be payd unto the sd Bernard Smith his Executors Administrators or assigns the sum of seven hundred pounds of good and lawful Money of England at three several payments that is to say Two hundred and thirty three pounds six shillings and eight pence thereof in hand at or before the sealing and delivering hereof the receipt whereof the sd Bernard Smith doth hereby acknowledge and confess and thereof and of every part & parcel thereof doth clearly acquit exonerate & discharge the sd Dean and Chapter [blank] by these presents other two hundred thirty three pounds six shillings and eight pence thereof when the sd whole organ or organs is or are brought into the sd Cathedral Church and ready for fitting up and two hundred and thirty three pounds six shillings and eight pence being the residue thereof and in full amount of the said sum of seven hundred pounds when the whole Organ is fitt up and in every respect finished according to the true intent and meaning of these articles. And further that the said Bernard Smith shall have and take to his own use benefit and charge the old Organ now belonging to the said Cathedral Church and all the Materialls thereunto belonging Provided the sd Bernard Smith shall not or do not remove take nor carry away the sd old Organ till the new organ be ready for fitting up as aforesaid.

And lastly whereas the pipes of the two fronts of the sd great Organ and the front pipes of the sd Chair Organ are to be painted and guilt according to the best way & made of painting & guilding of Organs at the proper cost & charges of the sd Bernard Smith. It is hereby agreed by and between the sd parties that if the sd Bernard Smith do well and sufficiently perform all the aforesaid works in making finishing and fitting up the sd new organ to the ample satisfaction and content of the sd Dean and Chapter That the said Dean and Chapter shall pay or cause to be payd unto the said Bernard Smith his Exrs admrs or assigns the sum of fifty pounds of good and lawfull money of England and in full satisfaction for the painting and guilding of the sd organ.

In witness whereof to the one part of these articles remaining with the sd Bernard Smith the sd Dean and Chapter have put this Chapter seal, and to the other part remaining with the sd Dean and Chapter the sd Bernard Smith hath put his hand & seal the day & year above written.

BER: SMITH
Signed sealed and delivered in the presence of
WILLIAM WILSON
JO. SIMPSON

Appendix 2: Stop-lists

a. The Father Smith organ and its subsequent alterations

A. As built with "additions" 1685/6

B. In MS. A.14 (1813 watermark)
Preliminary to England/Nicholls' work

Compass: FF, GG, AA - c3 (54 notes) with 7 extra pipes for ¼ tones. High pitch?

Great

Open Diopason (E front)		8
Open Diopason (W front)		8
Stop Diopason	(wood)	8
Princepall		4
Holfleut	(wood)	4
Quinta		2 ⅔
Super Octava		2
Small Quinta		1 ⅓
Mixtur (1)		IV
Sex quialtera		III
Cornet (c1 sharp)		IV
Trumpet		8

Great

R	Op.Diapason
L	Op.Diapason
L	Stop'd Do.
R	Principal
L	Flute
L	Twelfth
R	15th
R	22-Tierca
R	Forniture
L	Sesqualtera
R	Cornet
L	Trumpet

Chear

Stop Diopason	(wood)	8
Principall (front)		4
Holfleut	(wood)	4
Super Octava		2
Too an Twenty		1
Voise Humano		8

Choir

L	Stop'd Diapason
R	Dulciano (3)
L	Principal
L	Flute (3)
R	Flagalet: Dulc:Princ: (3)
R	15th
R	Voc Hermana

(wanted instead of this the Dulciana)

Swell

[Added by Jordan/Bridge 1748 (2)]
Compass: f to c3 (32 notes) with ¼ tones?

Open Diapason	8
Stop Diapason	8
Trumpet	8
Hautboy	8

Echoes

L	Op.
L	Stop'd Diapason
R	Trumpet
R	Hautboe
L	Cornet (4)

Notes

(1) MS Note says: 'Blockfleut is put in by the Mixtur of 3 rankes which is now 4 rankes, and the sexquialtera is put in that plas'; ie. the separate Blockfleut proposed in the 1683 contract was omitted.
(2) Though the contract was with Jordan, it was Mr. Bridge at the organ in 1748.

(3) By Snetzler, 1765, according to Buckingham

(4) By G.P.England , 1815, according to Buckingham (but a Cornet was inpre-1815 stoplist)

(5) Durham Advertiser: 25 Jan.1867

C. In Buckingham's Notebook 1823

Compass: GG, AA – e3 (57 notes)
¼ tones suppressed

Great

Double Diapason (24 pipes) (4)	16
Op. Diapason	8
Op. Diapason	8
St. Diapason	8
Principal	4
Flute	4
Twelfth	2⅔
Fifteenth	2
Nineteenth	1⅓
Mixtur	III
Sesquialtera	III
Cornet (c1)	III
Trumpet	8

Choir

St. Diapason	8
Dulciana (g, gr.bass)	8
Principal	4
Flute (metal)	4
Dula Principal (c, gr.bass)	4
Fifteenth	2
Cremona (c)	8

Swell

Compass extended up to e3 (36 notes) and,
in 1844, down to c (41 notes)

Open Diapason	8
St. Diapason	8
Principal (4)	4
Trumpet	8
Hautboy	8
Cornet (4)	III

Pedal

17 pull-downs, GG, AA to c. No pipes (4).
from 1844: double Pedal pipes:
GG, AA to g (24 notes)

D. As finally rebuilt 1866 (5)

Compass: Manuals C – g3 (56 notes)
Pedals C – g1 (32 notes)

Great

		Origin
Open Diapason (front)	8	Smith
Open Diapason (back)	8	Smith
Stopped Diapason (wood)	8	Smith
Clarabella (c1 + Postill bass)	8	Bishop 1844
Octave	4	Smith
Flute (wood, stopped)	4	Smith
Octave Quint	2⅔	Bishop 1844
Super Octave	2	Smith
Piccolo (wood)	2	Postill
Mixture	III	Bishop 1844
Sesquialtera	III	Bishop 1844
Trumpet	8	Jordan ?

Choir (new soundboard Bishop 1859)

Open Diapason (c)	8	Bishop 1859
Clarabella & St. Diapason	8	Bishop 1844
Dulciana	8	Bishop 1844
Viol di Gamba (c)	8	Bishop 1859
Octave	4	Smith
Flute (metal, stopped)	4	Snetzler
Dulcet	4	Snetzler
Super Octave	2	Smith
Cremona	8	Bishop 1847 + Postill bass

Swell

Bourdon	16	Postill
Open Diapason	8	pt. Jordan
Stopped Diapason (metal)	8	pt. Jordan
Belle-Gamba (c)	8	Postill
Octave	4	pt. England
Clarionette Flute (wood)	4	Postill
Octave Quint	2⅔	Postill
Super Octave	2	Postill
Mixture	IV	Postill
Trumpet	8	pt. Jordan ?
Hautboy	8	Bishop 1847
Clarion	4	Bishop 1844

Pedal

Open Wood	16 and 8	Bishop/Postill
Violon Wood	16 and 8	Postill
Posaune	16 and 8	Postill

b. The Father Willis organ: 1876

Further details online at <http://www.duresme.org.uk/CATH/willis.htm>

Of 55 speaking stops on five divisions, the new organ was thoroughly up-to-date, a first class creation of a singularly successful Victorian organ-builder. It is not altogether certain that the stop names below, from Hopkins & Rimbault (3rd Edition: 1877), are the exact original nomenclature.
The wind pressures given are those of the contemporary Salisbury Cathedral organ.

Pedal (C to f1, 30 notes). South and north sides.
Flues: 2", 2½", 3¾", 4"; Reeds: 9", 12"

1.	Open Diapason	32	wood	
2.	Open Diapason	16	wood	
3.	Open Diapason	16	metal	[north side case pipes]
4.	Violon	16	metal	[north side case pipes]
5.	Bourdon	16	wood	
6.	Octave	8	metal	
7.	Flute	8	wood	
8.	Mixture	IV	metal	12:15:19:22?
9.	Posaune	16	metal	
10.	Cornopean	8	metal	

Great (C to a3, 58 notes). South side.
Flues: 3½", 3⅞"; Reeds: 8"

11.	Open Diapason	16	metal	[south side case pipes]
12.	Open Diapason	8	metal	[large]
13.	Open Diapason	8	metal	[small]
14.	Gamba	8	metal	
15.	Stopped Diapason	8	wood	
16.	Claribel Flute	8	wood; 24 bass notes from No.15	
17.	Octave	4	metal	
18.	Harmonic Flute	4	metal	
19.	Twelfth	2⅔	metal	
20.	Fifteenth	2	metal	
21.	Piccolo	2	wood	
22.	Mixture	IV	metal	15:17:19:22
23.	Double Trumpet	16	metal	
24.	Cornopean	8	metal	
25.	Clarion	4	metal	

Swell enclosed (C to a3, 58 notes). North side.
4½" throughout

26.	Double Diapason	16	metal+wood	
27.	Open Diapason	8	metal	[large]
28.	Open Diapason	8	metal	[small]
29.	Lieblich Gedact	8	wood	
30.	Viol d'Amour	8	metal	
31.	Octave	4	metal	
32.	Harmonic Flute	4	metal	
33.	Fifteenth	2	metal	

34.	Piccolo	2	wood	
35.	Mixture	V	metal	12:15:17:19:22
36.	Oboe	8	metal	
37.	Vox Humana	8	metal	
38.	Contra Fagotto	16	metal	
39.	Trumpet	8	metal	
40.	Clarion	4	metal	

Choir unenclosed (C to a3, 58 notes). North side.
2⅞" throughout

41.	Lieblich Gedact	16	metal+wood
42.	Lieblich Gedact	8	metal+wood
43.	Flauto Traverso	8	wood
44.	Salicional	8	metal
45.	Vox Angelica TC	8	metal
46.	Gemshorn	4	metal
47.	Lieblich Gedact	4	metal
48.	Flauto Traverso	4	wood
49.	Corno di Bassetto	8	metal

Solo unenclosed (C to a3, 58 notes). South side.
Flues + orch'l reeds: 4"; Tubas:bass 15⅜", treble 18½"

50.	Harmonic Flute	8	metal
51.	Concert Harmonic Fl.	4	metal
52.	Orchestral Oboe	8	metal
53.	Corno di Bassetto	8	metal
54.	Tuba	8	metal
55.	Clarion	4	metal

Couplers

i)	Great to Pedals	vi)	Swell to Great Octave
ii)	Swell to Pedals	vii)	Swell to Great Sub Octave
iii)	Choir to Pedals	viii)	Choir to Great
iv)	Solo to Pedals	ix)	Solo to Great
v)	Swell to Great Unison	x)	Tremulant to Swell

4 composition pedals to Great   Reversible Great to Pedals lever
3 composition pedals to Swell   Lever Swell Pedal (mechanical link)
3 composition pedals to Pedal

All 55 ranks were independent and complete in themselves, save for the shared bass of the Great Stopped Diapason and Claribel Flute.

The key and stop action was tubular pneumatic; the coupling and swell pedal control mechanical. The console was on the South side, where it has remained since.

Wind supplied by six large bellows, blown by three hydraulic engines

Cost £3150

c. The re-buildings by Harrison & Harrison

i. 1905

The organ consists of four manuals, C to a3, 58 notes, and pedals, C to f1, 30 notes, and completed will contain 73 speaking stops and 17 couplers, etc., making a total of 90 drawstops.   The stops marked * are prepared for only.

Pedal

1.	Double Open Diapason	32	1876	wood
2.	Open Diapason	16	1876	wood
*3.	Open Diapason	16	-	18 from No. 1
4.	Open Diapason	16	1876	metal: north front
5.	Dulciana	16	1876	north front: Violon re-named
6.	Bourdon	16	1876	
*7.	Principal	8	-	18 from No. 2
8.	Octave	8	1876	
9.	Flute	8	1876	
10.	Mixture (12.15.19.22)	IV	1876	
*11.	Contra Bombard	32	-	
*12.	Bombard	16	-	18 from No. 11
13.	Ophicleide	16	1876	Posaune re-named
14.	Cornopean	8	1876	

I Solo to Pedal
II Swell to Pedal
III Great to Pedal
IV Choir to Pedal

Great

15.	Double Open Diapason	16	1876	south front
*16.	Contra Clarabella	16	-	
17.	Open Diapason	8	1876	large
18.	Open Diapason	8	1876	small
19.	Stopped Diapason	8	1876	
20.	Gamba	8	1876	
*21.	Hohlflöte	8	-	
22.	Claribel Flute	8	1876	bottom 24 from No. 19
23.	Principal	4	1876	
24.	Harmonic Flute	4	1876	
*25.	Suabe Flute	4	-	
26.	Twelfth	2⅔	1876	
27.	Fifteenth	2	1876	
28.	Piccolo	2	1876	
29.	Mixture (15.17.19.22)	IV	1876	
30.	Double Trumpet	16	1876	
31.	Posaune	8	1876/1905	hm trebles: Cornopean re-named
*32.	Horn	8	-	
33.	Clarion	4	1876/1905	harmonic trebles

V Solo to Great
VI Swell to Great
VII Choir to Great

Swell (enclosed)

34.	Double Diapason	16	1876	
35.	Open Diapason	8	1876	large
36.	Open Diapason	8	1876	small
37.	Lieblich Gedeckt	8	1876	
38.	Viole d'Amour	8	1876	
39.	Vox Angelica [Tenor C]	8	1876	previously on Choir
40.	Octave	4	1876	
41.	Harmonic Flute	4	1876	
42.	Super Octave	2	1876	
43.	Mixture (12.15.17.19.22)	V	1876	
44.	Oboe	8	1876	
45.	Vox Humana	8	1876	
46.	Contra Fagotto	16	1876	
47.	Trumpet	8	1876/1905	harmonic trebles
48.	Clarion	4	1876/1905	harmonic trebles

VIII Tremulant

Choir (enclosed)

49.	Lieblich Gedeckt	16	1876	
*50.	Open Diapason	8	-	
51.	Lieblich Gedeckt	8	1876	
52.	Flauto Traverso	8	1876	
*53.	Viola da Gamba	8	-	
54.	Salicional	8	1876	
55.	Gemshorn	4	1876	
56.	Lieblich Gedeckt	4	1876	
57.	Flauto Traverso	4	1876	
58.	Harmonic Piccolo	2	1876	previously Swell Piccolo
*59.	Dulciana Mixture (12.19.22)	III	-	
60.	Clarinet	8	1876	Corno di Bassetto re-named

IX Swell to Choir

Solo (unenclosed)

*61.	Contra Viola	16	-	
*62.	Viole d'Orchestre	8	-	
*63.	Viole Céleste	8	-	
*64.	Cornet de Violes (8.10.12.15)	IV	-	
65.	Harmonic Flute	8	1876	
66.	Concert Flute	4	1876	
*67.	Cor Anglais	16	-	
68.	Corno di Bassetto	8	1876	
69.	Orchestral Oboe	8	1876	
*70.	Trombone	16	-	
*71.	Tromba	8	-	

72.	Tuba		8	1876/ ?1905	?	harmonic
73.	Tuba Clarion		4	1876/ ?1905	?	harmonic

* *X Tremulant (to Nos. 61 to 69)*

XI Solo Octave (to Nos. 61 to 71)
XII Swell to Solo
* *XIII Great Reeds to Solo*

The Solo Organ remains unenclosed, but when completed, Nos. 61 to 71 will be enclosed in a swell-box and will each have a compass of 70 pipes *[However, only the Cor Anglais was given a 70 note compass in 1935].*

Combination Couplers
XIV Pedal and Accompaniment to Solo Pistons
XV Pedal and Accompaniment to Swell Pistons
XVI Great and Pedal Combinations Coupled
XVII Pedal and Accompaniment to Choir Pistons

Accessories
Six Combination Pistons to Great (and Pedal) Organ stops
Six Combination Pedals to Pedal (and Great) Organ stops
Six Combination Pistons to Swell Organ stops
Four Combination Pistons to Choir Organ stops
Six Combination Pistons to Solo Organ stops
Reversible Piston to "Great to Pedal" coupler
Four stop-control switches for changeable combinations
Three balanced Crescendo Pedals

Wind Pressures
Pedal Organ: Flue-work 1½ inches to 4½ inches, reeds 12 inches and 15 inches
Great Organ: Flue-work 4 inches, reeds 7 inches
Swell Organ: Flue-work, Oboe and Vox Humana 3½ inches, other reeds 7 inches
Choir Organ: 2¼ inches
Solo Organ: Flue-work and orchestral reed 6 inches, Trombas 16 ft. and 8 ft.
   (enclosed) 12 inches, Tubas: 8 ft. and 4 ft. (unenclosed) 15 and 20 inches

The Pedal-board is radiating and concave.

The three Crescendo Pedals (on the balanced principle) are placed side by side to the right of the centre of the knee-board.

The Draw-stops are at an angle of 45° to the key-boards. The Stop-handles are of solid ivory, the speaking stops being lettered in black and the Couplers in red. The latter are grouped with the speaking-stops of the divisions they augment. The Thumb-Pistons are of solid ivory.

By means of the Combination Couplers Nos. XIV, XV and XVII, the pistons provide suitable Pedal basses at will; and the Great organ pistons and Pedal organ combination pedals act either independently or can be coupled together by drawing No. XVI.

The Pitch, being but slightly sharper than the new Philharmonic (C = 517 vibrations per second at 60 degrees F), has not been altered.

All the metal pipes are of rich spotted metal, excepting the 16 ft octaves of Nos. 4, 5 and 15, which stand in the two fronts and are richly decorated.

[The above information, from a contemporary leaflet, does not specify that a new tubular-pneumatic action was used for the south side of the organ (Great and Solo and some Pedal), but electro-pneumatic action for the north side]

Willis's North case front, decorated by Clayton & Bell, wood carving by Roddis of Birmingham [© RDH]

ii 1935

The organ consists of four manuals, 77 speaking stops and 20 couplers;
compass C to a3, 58 notes; Pedal compass: C to f1, 30 notes.

Pedal

1.	Double Open Wood	32	1876	
2.	Open Wood I	16	1876	
3.	Open Wood II	16	1876/1935	18 from No. 1
4.	Open Diapason	16	1876	north side front pipes
5.	Dulciana	16	1876	north side front pipes
6.	Bourdon	16	1876	
7.	Violone	16	1935	from Solo (No. 63)
8.	Octave Wood	8	1876/1935	18 from No. 2
9.	Principal	8	1876	
10.	Flute	8	1876	
11.	Super Octave Wood	4	1876/1935	18 from Nos. 2 and 8
12.	Mixture (12.15.19.22)	IV	1876	
13.	Double Ophicleide	32	1935	18 from No. 14: metal
14.	Ophicleide	16	1935	
15.	Trombone	16	1876	Ophicleide re-named
16.	Cor Anglais	16	1935	from Solo (No. 71)
17.	Tromba	8	1876	Cornopean re-named

I Choir to Pedal   II Great to Pedal   III Swell to Pedal   IV Solo to Pedal

Choir (enclosed)

18.	Lieblich Bourdon	16	1876
19.	Open Diapason	8	1935
20.	Lieblich Gedeckt	8	1876
21.	Flauto Traverso	8	1876
22.	Viola da Gamba	8	1935
23.	Salicional	8	1876
24.	Gemshorn	4	1876
25.	Lieblich Flute	4	1876
26.	Flauto Traverso	4	1876
27.	Harmonic Piccolo	2	1876
28.	Dulciana Mixture (15.19.22)	III	1935
29.	Clarinet	8	1876

V Swell to Choir   VI Solo to Choir

Great

30.	Double Open Diapason	16	1876	south front pipes
31.	Contra Clarabella	16	1876/1935	wood: bottom 12 from No. 6
32.	Open Diapason I	8	1935	leathered
33.	Open Diapason II	8	1876	large Open Diapason of 1876
34.	Open Diapason III	8	1876	small Open Diapason of 1876
35.	Open Diapason IV	8	1935	
36.	Gamba	8	1876	

37.	Stopped Diapason	8	1876	
38.	Claribel Flute	8	1876	bottom 24 from No. 37
39.	Octave	4	1876	
40.	Principal	4	1935	
41.	Harmonic Flute	4	1876	
42.	Octave Quint	2⅔	1876	
43.	Super Octave	2	1876	
44.	Mixture (15.17.19.22)	IV	1876	
45.	Contra Posaune	16	1876	
46.	Posaune	8	1876/1905	harmonic trebles
47.	Clarion	4	1876/1905	harmonic trebles

VII Reeds on Choir
VIII Choir to Great   IX Swell to Great   X Solo to Great

Swell (enclosed)

48.	Double Diapason	16	1876	
49.	Open Diapason I	8	1876	
50.	Open Diapason II	8	1876	
51.	Lieblich Gedeckt	8	1876	
52.	Viole d'Amour	8	1876	
53.	Vox Angelica (Ten. C)	8	1876	
54.	Principal	4	1876	
55.	Harmonic Flute	4	1876	
56.	Fifteenth	2	1876	
57.	Mixture (12.15.17.19.22)	V	1876	
58.	Oboe	8	1876	
59.	Vox Humana	8	1876	

XI Tremulant

60.	Double Trumpet	16	1876	Contra Fagotto re-named
61.	Trumpet	8	1876/1905	harmonic trebles
62.	Clarion	4	1876/1905	harmonic trebles

XII Solo to Swell

Solo (Nos. 63 to 75 enclosed)

63.	Contra Viola	16	1935	
64.	Viole d'Orchestre	8	1935	
65.	Viole Celeste	8	1935	full compass
66.	Viole Octaviante	4	1935	
67.	Cornet de Violes (10.12.15)	III	1935	
68.	Harmonic Flute	8	1876/1935	rescaled
69.	Concert Flute	4	1876/1935	rescaled
70.	Harmonic Piccolo	2	1876/1935	previously Great Piccolo
71.	Cor Anglais	16	1935	
72.	Corno di Bassetto	8	1876	
73.	Orchestral Oboe	8	1876	

XIII Tremulant

Solo (con't)

74.	French Horn	8	1935	harmonic
75.	Orchestral Tuba	8	1935	harmonic
76.	Tuba	8	1876	harmonic: revoiced 1905 and/or 1935
77.	Tuba Clarion	4	1876	harmonic: revoiced 1905 and/or 1935

XIV Octave   XV Sub Octave   XVI Unison Off
No. 71 has an extra octave of pipes at the top for use with Nos. XIV and XVI.

Combination couplers

XVII Pedal to Choir Pistons   XVIII Great and Pedal Combinations Coupled
XIX Pedal to Swell Pistons   XX Pedal to Solo Pistons

Accessories

Nine combination foot pistons and one adjustable piston to the Pedal organ
Five combination pistons and one adjustable piston to the Choir organ
Eight combination pistons and one adjustable piston to the Great organ
Seven combination pistons and one adjustable piston to the Swell organ
Eight combination pistons and one adjustable piston to the Solo organ
Compound switch to the adjustable pistons
Cancelling switches to the whole organ, Great organ, and Swell organ
Foot piston for "Doubles off"
Reversible pistons to No. 14 and No. 15
Reversible foot piston to Great to Pedal
Reversible pistons to Great to Pedal, Swell to Great, and Solo to Great
Three balanced crescendo pedals to the Choir, Swell and Solo organs.

Wind pressures

Pedal: Flue-work 1½ inches to 6 inches; reeds 6 inches, 12 inches and 20 inches.
Choir: 2¾ inches.   Great: flue-work 4 inches and 5 inches; reeds 7 inches.
Swell: Flue-work, Oboe and Vox Humana 3½ inches;   chorus reeds, 7 inches.
Solo: Flue-work and orchestral reeds, 6 inches;   Tubas and French Horn, 20 inches.

The drawstop jambs are at an angle of 45 degrees to the keyboards. The stop handles have solid ivory fronts, the speaking stops being lettered in black and the couplers etc. in red. The couplers are grouped with the speaking stops of the departments they augment. The combination pistons have solid ivory heads.

The pitch is C = 528 vibrations at 59 degrees F.

The blowing is by "Discus" fans and 3 electric motors, by Messrs. Watkins and Watson of London

[The above, from contemporary publicity, does not specify that the tubular-pneumatic action to the south side and electro-pneumatic action to the north side of the organ were retained]

iii. 1970

The manual compass is C to a3, 58 notes: the pedal C to f1, 30 notes

Pedal

1.	Double Open Wood	32	1876	30	
2.	Open Wood I	16	1876	30	
3.	Open Wood II (18 from No. 1)	16	1876/1935	12	
4.	Open Diapason	16	1876	30	north side front
5.	Violone [previously called Dulciana]	16	1876	30	north side front
6.	Dulciana	16	1935/1970	30	south choir aisle front
					part from 1935 Ch. Op. Diap.
7.	Bourdon	16	1876	30	
8.	Contra Viola (from No. 84)	16	1935	-	previously Violone
9.	Octave Wood (18 from No. 2)	8	1876/1935	12	
10.	Principal	8	1876	30	
11.	Cello (18 from No. 5)	8	1876/1935/1970	12	part from 1935 Ch. Op. Diap.
12.	Dulciana (18 from No. 6)	8	1935/1970	12	from 1935 Ch. Viola da G.
13.	Flute	8	1876	30	
14.	Twelfth	5⅓	1876/1970	30	part from 1876 Pedal Mix.
15.	Super Octave Wood (18 from Nos. 2 & 9)	4	1876/1935	12	
16.	Octave Cello (18 from Nos. 5 & 11)	4	1935/1970	12	part from 1935 Ch Op. Diap
17.	Twenty Second	2	1876/1970	30	part from 1876 Pedal Mix.
18.	Mixture (19.22.26.29)	IV	1876/1970	120	remade
19.	Double Ophicleide (18 from No. 21)	32	1935	12	in Bombarde division*
20.	Double Trombone (18 from No. 22)	32	1876/1970	12	bottom 12 notes new
21.	Ophicleide	16	1935	30	in Bombarde division*
22.	Trombone	16	1876	30	
23.	Cor Anglais (from No. 92)	16	1935	-	
24.	Tromba	8	1876	30	
25.	Cornett	4	1970	30	

I Choir to Pedal   II Great to Pedal   III Swell to Pedal   IV Solo to Pedal

Positive (on Choir keys)

26.	Flûte à Cheminée	8	1970	58	
27.	Quintade	8	1970	58	
28.	Prestant	4	1970	58	
29.	Flute Ouverte	4	1970	58	
30.	Doublette	2	1970	58	
31.	Sesquialtera (12.17)	II	1970	116	
32.	Larigot	1⅓	1970	58	
33.	Octavin	1	1970	58	
34.	Octave Tierce	⅘	1970	58	
35.	Cymbale (26.29.33)	III	1970	174	
36.	Dulzian	16	1970	58	
37.	Trompette	8	1970	58	

V Positive on Solo   VI Positive on Great

Choir (enclosed)

38.	Bourdon	16	1876	58	
39.	Viole d'Amour	8	1876	58	previously on **Swell**
40.	Gedeckt	8	1876	58	
41.	Flauto Traverso	8	1876	58	
42.	Gemshorn	4	1876	58	
43.	Stopped Flute	4	1876	58	
44.	Flauto Traverso	4	1876	58	
45.	Nazard	2⅔	1970	58	
46.	Piccolo	2	1876	58	
47.	Tierce	1⅗	1970	58	
48.	Dulciana Mixture (15.19.22)	III	1935	174	
49.	Clarinet	8	1876	58	

VII Swell to Choir   VIII Solo to Choir   IX Bombarde Tubas on Choir

Great

50.	Double Open Diapason	16	1876	58	south side front
51.	Contra Clarabella (12 from No. 7)	16	1876/1935	46	
52.	Open Diapason I	8	1935	58	
53.	Open Diapason II	8	1876	58	
54.	Open Diapason III	8	1876	58	
55.	Open Diapason IV	8	1935	58	
56.	Gamba	8	1876	58	
57.	Stopped Diapason	8	1876	58	
58.	Claribel Flute (24 from No. 57)	8	1876	34	
59.	Octave	4	1876	58	
60.	Principal	4	1935	58	
61.	Harmonic Flute	4	1876	58	
62.	Octave Quint	2⅔	1876	58	
63.	Super Octave	2	1876	58	
64.	Mixture (19.22.26.29)	IV	1876/1970	232	some new pipes in 1970
65.	Scharf (29.33.36)	III	1970	174	
66.	Contra Posaune	16	1876	58	
67.	Posaune	8	1876/1905	58	harmonic trebles
68.	Clarion	4	1876/1905	58	harmonic trebles

X Reeds on Choir   XI Choir to Great   XII Swell to Great   XIII Solo to Great

Swell (enclosed)

69.	Double Diapason	16	1876	58	
70.	Open Diapason I	8	1876	58	
71.	Open Diapason II	8	1876	58	
72.	Lieblich Gedeckt	8	1876	58	
73.	Salicional	8	1876	58	previously on Choir
74.	Vox Angelica (Tenor C)	8	1876	46	
75.	Principal	4	1876	58	
76.	Harmonic Flute	4	1876	58	
77.	Fifteenth	2	1876	58	
78.	Mixture (12.15.17.19.22)	IV/V	1876	274	
79.	Oboe	8	1876	58	

80.	Vox Humana	8	1876	58	

XIV Tremulant

81.	Double Trumpet	16	1876	58	
82.	Trumpet	8	1876/1905	58	harmonic trebles
83.	Clarion	4	1876/1905	58	harmonic trebles

XV Solo to Swell

Solo (Nos. 84 to 96 enclosed)

84.	Contra Viola	16	1935	58	
85.	Viole d'Orchestre	8	1935	58	
86.	Viole Celeste	8	1935	58	
87.	Viole Octaviante	4	1935	58	
88.	Cornet de Violes (10.12.15)	III	1935	174	
89.	Harmonic Flute	8	1876/1935	58	
90.	Concert Flute	4	1876/1935	58	
91.	Harmonic Piccolo	2	1876/1935	58	
92.	Cor Anglais	16	1935	70	
93.	Corno di Bassetto	8	1876	58	
94.	Orchestral Oboe	8	1876	58	

XVI Tremulant

95.	French Horn	8	1935	58	
96.	Orchestral Tuba	8	1935	58	
97.	Tuba	8	1876	58} in Bombarde division *	
98.	Tuba Clarion	4	1876	58} revoiced 1905 &/or 1935	

XVII Octave   XVIII Sub Octave   XIX Unison Off
No. 92 has an extra octave of pipes in the treble for use with Nos. XVII and XIX

Combination couplers
XX Pedal to Choir Pistons [replaced in 1982 by Generals on Swell foot pistons]
XXI Pedal to Swell Pistons   XXII Great and Pedal Combinations Coupled

* The drawstops of Nos. 19, 21, 97 and 98 are grouped as the Bombarde Division.

Accessories
Nine foot pistons to the Pedal Organ [later 10]
Four pistons to the Positive Organ (also controlling Choir stops)
Four pistons to the Choir Organ (also controlling Positive stops) [later 10 for both divisions]
Nine pistons to the Great Organ [later 10]
Nine pistons to the Swell Organ (duplicated by foot pistons) [later 10]
Nine pistons to the Solo Organ, with fixed combinations [later 10, adjustable]
Four general pistons [later 10]
The above pistons (except those for Solo Organ) are adjustable by switch [no longer applies]
One extra piston to each department, adjustable by setter piston
'Compound' piston, operating all instantly adjustable pistons together [later removed]
Reversible pistons: I-IX, XI-XIII, XV; 22
Reversible foot pistons: I, II, XII, XXI, XXII
One piston for Posaune 8 on Choir (Nos. X and 67) [later for Orch.Tuba]
One piston for Posaune 16 on Pedal (Nos. 1, X and 66) [later for Tuba]
One reversible piston for Tubas on Choir (Nos. IX, 97 and 98) [later removed]

Pedal Cancel foot piston

General Cancel piston

[Additional piston facilities were provided in 1982 and 1994, and a setter mechanism (by capture system) installed: at first dual, later 18x memory (to all departmental and general pistons)

Balanced expression pedals to the Choir, Swell and Solo Organs

The actions are electro-pneumatic throughout

The blowing equipment [3 blowers] and humidifiers are by Messrs. Watkins & Watson Ltd.

The console today [© RDH]

iv. The Organ Today

The organ was overhauled in stages between 1993 and 2001.

PEDAL ORGAN

	1.	Double Open Wood	32
	2.	Open Wood I	16
†	3.	Open Wood II (from 1)	16
	4.	Open Diapason	16
	5.	Violone	16
*	6.	Dulciana	16
	7.	Bourdon	16
†	8.	Contra Viola (from 84)	16
†	9.	Octave Wood (from 2)	8
	10.	Principal	8
*	11.	Violoncello (from 5)	8
*	12.	Dulciana (from 6)	8
	13.	Flute	8
	14.	Twelfth (from 5)	5⅓
†	15.	Super Octave Wood (from 2)	4
	16.	Fifteenth (1996)	4
*	17.	Twenty Second	2
**	18.	Mixture 19.22.26.29	IV
†	19.	Double Ophicleide (from 21)	32
*	20.	Double Trombone (from 22)	32
†	21.	Ophicleide	16
	22.	Trombone	16
†	23.	Cor Anglais (from 92)	16
	24.	Tromba	8
*	25.	Cornett	4

I Choir to Pedal   II Great to Pedal
III Swell to Pedal   IV Solo to Pedal

POSITIVE ORGAN

*	26.	Flûte à Cheminée	8
*	27.	Quintade	8
*	28.	Prestant	4
*	29.	Flûte Ouverte	4
*	30.	Doublette	2
*	31.	Sesquialtera	II
*	32.	Larigot	1⅓
*	33.	Octavin	1
*	34.	Octave Tierce	⅘
*	35.	Cymbale 26.29.33	III
*	36.	Dulzian	16
*	37.	Trompette	8

V Positive on Great VI Positive on Solo

CHOIR ORGAN (enclosed)

	38.	Bourdon	16
	39.	Gedeckt	8
	40.	Flauto Traverso	8
	41.	Viole d'Amour	8
	42.	Gemshorn	4
	43.	Stopped Flute	4
	44.	Flauto Traverso	4
*	45.	Nazard	2⅔
	46.	Piccolo	2
*	47.	Tierce	1⅗
†	48.	Dulciana Mixture 15.19.22	III
	49.	Clarinet	8

VII Tremulant (2001)
VIII Swell to Choir
IX Solo to Choir
X Bombarde Tubas on Choir

GREAT ORGAN

	50.	Double Open Diapason	16
†	51.	Contra Clarabella (12 from 7)	16
†	52.	Open Diapason I	8
	53.	Open Diapason II	8
	54.	Open Diapason III	8
†	55.	Open Diapason IV	8
	56.	Gamba	8
	57.	Stopped Diapason	8
	58.	Claribel Flute (24 from 57)	8
	59.	Octave	4
†	60.	Principal	4
	61.	Harmonic Flute	4
	62.	Octave Quint	2⅔
	63.	Super Octave	2
**	64.	Mixture 19.22.26.29	IV
*	65.	Scharf 26.29.33	III
	66.	Contra Posaune	16
	67.	Posaune	8
	68.	Clarion	4

XI Reeds on Choir   XII Choir to Great
XIII Swell to Great   XIV Solo to Great

SWELL ORGAN

69.	Double Diapason	16
70.	Open Diapason I	8
71.	Open Diapason II	8
72.	Lieblich Gedeckt	8
73.	Salicional	8
74.	Vox Angelica (tenor c)	8
55.	Principal	4
76.	Harmonic Flute	4
77.	Fifteenth	2
78.	Mixture 12.15.17.19.22	V
79.	Oboe	8
80.	Vox Humana	8
XV	Tremulant	
81.	Double Trumpet	16
82.	Trumpet	8
83.	Clarion	4
XVI	Solo to Swell	

SOLO ORGAN (84-96 enclosed)

†	84.	Contra Viola	16
†	85.	Viole d'Orchestre	8
†	86.	Viole Céleste	8
†	87.	Viole Octaviante	4
†	88.	Cornet de Violes 10.12.15	III
	89.	Harmonic Flute	8
	90.	Concert Flute	4
	91.	Harmonic Piccolo	2
†	92.	Cor Anglais	16
	93.	Corno di Bassetto	8
	94.	Orchestral Oboe	8
	XVII	Tremulant	
†	95.	French Horn	8
†	96.	Orchestral Tuba	8
	97.	Tuba	8
	98.	Tuba Clarion	4

XVIII Octave XIX Sub Octave
XX Unison Off
(No 92 has an extra octave of pipes in the treble

COMBINATION COUPLERS

XXI	Generals on Swell foot pistons
XXII	Pedal to Swell pistons
XXIII	Great and Pedal Combinations coupled

† 1935 additions
* 1970 additions
** Revised 1970
☐ Stops 19, 21, 97 and 98 are grouped as the Bombarde Division

The manual compass is 58 notes
The pedal compass is 30 notes
The actions are electro-pneumatic

ACCESSORIES (1994)

Ten foot pistons to the Pedal Organ
Ten pistons to the Choir and Positive Organs
Ten pistons to the Great Organ
Ten pistons to the Swell Organ
   (duplicated by foot pistons)
Ten pistons to the Solo Organ
Ten general pistons and general cancel
Reversible pistons: I-VI, VIII, IX, XII – XIV, XVI, XXII, XXIII; 1, 20, 22
Reversible foot pistons: II, III, XIII, 1
Piston for Solo Orchestral Tuba (96)
Piston for Solo Tuba (97)
Reversible pistons for Full Organ I and II
Pedal cancel foot piston
512 general and 16 divisional piston
   memories (2014)
Balanced expression pedals to the Choir,
   Swell and Solo Organs

Mixture compositions

Pedal Mixture:	19.22.26.29 throughout	
Postive Cymbale:	C	26.29.33
	A#	22.26.29
	g#	19.22.26
	f1#	15.19.22
	e2	12.15.19
	d3	12.12.15
Choir Mixture:	C	15.19.22
	c1	8.12.15
Great Mixture	C	19.22.26.29
	f#	15.19.22.26
	f1#	12.15.19.22
	f2#	8.12.15.19
	f3#	8.12.12.15
Great Scharf	C	26.29.33
[altered 2001]	f#	22.26.29
	f1#	19.22.26
	f2#	15.19.22
	c3#	12.15.19
	f3	8.12.15
Swell Mixture:	C	12.15.17.19.22
	c1	1.8.12.15.17
	f2#	1.8.12.15
Solo Cornet:	10.12.15 throughout	

Wind pressures

Pedal: Flues 2½ – 5 in ; Trombone 12 in
Choir: 2¾ in;   Positive 3 in
Great: Flues 4 in & 5 in; reeds 7½ in
Swell: chorus reeds (Nos. 81-83) 7 in ; remainder 3½ in
Solo: Tuba and French Horn 20 in; remainder 5⅞ in
Bombarde: Tubas (Nos. 97 & 98) 19¾ in; Pedal (Nos. 19 & 21) 21 in

Appendix 3 :
Masters of the Choristers and Organists

Masters of the Choristers (and, ipso facto, Organists)

1535	John Brimley
1576	William Browne
1588	Robert Masterman
1589	William Smith
1599	William Browne
1608	Edward Smith
1612	Francis Dodshon
1613	Richard Hutchinson

Masters of the Choristers and Organists

1661	John Foster
1677	Alexander Shaw (Organist only)
1681	William Greggs
1711	James Heseltine
1763	Thomas Ebdon
1811	Charles Clarke
1814	William Henshaw
1862	Philip Armes
1907	Arnold Culley
1933	John Dykes Bower
1936	Conrad Eden
1974	Richard Lloyd
1985	James Lancelot

Sub-Organists

1904	William Ellis
1918	Basil Maine
1919	Cyril Maude
1968	Bruce Cash
1973	Alan Thurlow
1980	David Hill
1981	Ian Shaw
1991	Keith Wright
2011	Francesca Massey

Assistant Organists

2009	Oliver Brett
2012	David Ratnanayagam

NOTES